CHINA
Our Pacific Neighbour

CHINA
Our Pacific Neighbour

by
Brian Evans
and
Agnes Yu

Illustrations
by
Yu Chao and Wang Jue

REIDMORE BOOKS INC.
Edmonton, Alberta, Canada

BRIAN EVANS

Dr. Evans is currently a Professor of History at the University of Alberta, and Associate Vice President (Academic) International Affairs. He received a bachelor's degree in history from the University of Alberta, and a doctorate, also in history, from the School of Oriental and African Studies, University of London, England. Brian Evans spent a year in Beijing acting as Cultural Counselor at the Canadian Embassy, and has traveled extensively throughout Asia, as well as the Commonwealth of Independent States, Africa, and South America.

AGNES YINLING YU

Dr. Yu currently works for the Edmonton Public School Board as a Consultant in ESL and Psychology. Born in Hong Kong, Agnes Yu received her education in Hong Kong, Canada, and Mexico. She has traveled and conducted ethnographic research in various parts of the world, including China, Mexico, France, and Canada. Professionally, Agnes Yu is an educator, psychologist, and researcher with a special interest in immigrant and minority groups, cross-cultural communication, and multicultural education. Agnes Yu is an active member of the Chinese community.

YU CHAO and WANG JUE

Mrs. Yu Chao and her husband Wang Jue are currently visiting scholars in the Faculty of Extension, University of Alberta. They received their bachelor's degrees at the Shandong Fine Arts Institute. Mrs. Yu has worked as a fine arts editor for Shandong Provincial Publishers. Mr. Wang was a fine arts teacher at the Shandong Fine Arts Institute for six years. Their works have been exhibited in many countries, including China and Japan. They have both received several national awards from the People's Republic of China. Together, they have published more than 20 books. They are now living in Edmonton.

Reidmore Books wishes to thank the following people for their helpful suggestions:

Shelly Bryan
Consultant
Edmonton, Alberta

Dr. Charles Burton
Department of Politics
Brock University
St. Catharines, Ontario

Dr. Ron Keith
Political Science Department
University of Calgary
Calgary, Alberta

Kathy Briner
St. Mary's Elementary School
Edmonton, Alberta

Student Reviewers:

Kimberley Hough
Edmonton, AB

Clay Shalagan
Edmonton, AB

REIDMORE BOOKS INC.
Suite 1200 Energy Square
10109 - 106 Street
Edmonton, Alberta T5J 3L7

Canadian Cataloguing in Publication Data

Evans, Brian L., 1932-

    China, our Pacific Neighbour

    ISBN 0-919091-47-4

1. Canada - Foreign relations - China - Juvenile literature.
2. China - Foreign relations - Canada - Juvenile literature. I. Yu, Agnes, Yinling, 1947 - II. Title.

FC251.C6E92 1990   j327.71051   C90-91563-3
F1029.5.C6E92 1990

printed and bound in Canada

Contents

Introduction

Learning is like rowing upstream

Not to advance is to fall behind

—Old Chinese Saying

Why Study China?

Have you ever seen a panda bear, eaten rice, flown a kite, or visited a Chinatown? Does anyone in your home drink tea or wear silk clothing? If your answer to any of these questions is yes, then you now know something about the things China has shared, through trade, tourism or immigration with Canadians like you.

Learning about China is important to Canadian students because the relationship between Canada and China is growing stronger over time. As the links between countries develop, it is important that the people in those countries learn more about each other.

This text will give you the chance to learn about China's past, Chinese **customs** and **traditions**, and changes that China has experienced and is still experiencing. You will also learn about China's geography, history and government, and the ways in which these things affect how Chinese people meet their daily needs.

As you study China, keep in mind that there are similarities and differences in the ways Canadians and Chinese meet their needs. As in any relationship, similarities start the relationship, and differences keep it interesting!

THINK ABOUT IT

1. When we study the words of people, we can learn about the things they consider important. At the top of this page is an old Chinese saying. This saying is one example of traditional Chinese beliefs. What does this saying tell you about the value of learning or education as seen by the Chinese people?

2. Preview this text by reading the sayings at the top of each chapter page. With a partner, discuss what each of these sayings tells you about the Chinese people's way of looking at the world. Record your ideas about things which the Chinese people appear to value. After you have completed your study of China, you will be returning to this activity to see how closely your original impressions of China match with your final impressions.

China Within the World

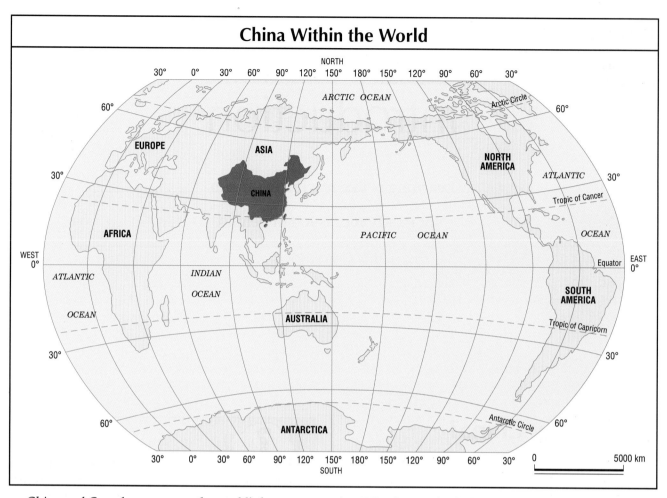

China and Canada are among the world's largest countries. Why do you think the Pacific Ocean might be important to China?

In the modern world, countries need to share with each other. They share knowledge, technology, and ways of meeting their needs. In sharing, we learn about the similarities and differences between us—Canada—and China—our **Pacific Rim** neighbour.

Getting Ready to Read

Each chapter in this book begins with a **Chapter Focus** that helps you to organize the information you will read in the chapter.

At the end of each chapter you will find a section called **A Look Back** to help you remember the main ideas. **A Look Ahead** introduces you to some of the main ideas in the following chapter.

Questions and **Activities** will help you try out your new knowledge, and think about the ideas presented.

Mini Studies and special features will give you added information as you read through the book.

You will find a number of words in bold type in *China: Our Pacific Neighbour*. These may be words you have not seen or used before. These words are defined in a **Glossary** at the end of the book. Here, you will also find the **Pronunciation Guide**. It will help you to pronounce the Chinese words in this book.

There are five different icons throughout the text: **Research**, **Reading Maps**, **Think About It**, **Let's Talk About It**, and **Sharing**. The icons focus on a special question or idea that is in the chapter.

Icon Guide

There are different ways of researching, organizing, and sharing information. As you use this book, the icons will guide you to new ideas, new thoughts, and new activities.

RESEARCH

You will be doing some extra reading, interviewing, questioning, and drawing conclusions about a particular topic.

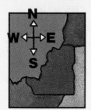

READING MAPS

This icon is near a map. Maps in this book give you information about land forms, boundaries, population, and other aspects of China. The icon includes an activity to help you understand the map it is near.

THINK ABOUT IT

You will compare, decide about or evaluate information you have read. Sometimes you will be asked to work with a partner or a group.

LET'S TALK ABOUT IT

You will discuss, debate, or plan presentations. You may be working on your own, with a partner, or in a group.

SHARING

You will examine the ways that China and other Pacific Rim neighbours share goods, services, ideas, and lifestyles with Canada.

We hope you will enjoy exploring how people live in China, and celebrating the friendship between Canada and China, our Pacific Rim neighbour.

This Chinese girl is visiting a museum. All of the objects on display are from China, and represent special aspects of Chinese life. Do you recognize any of the objects in the picture? Can you name other things for which China is well-known? In your notebook, record this information. Share your list with a partner and add new ideas to your notebook. When you have completed your study of China, look back at the original list you made. What new information can you add?

CHAPTER 1

Canadians from China

Abroad, we look at a person's clothes

At home, we look at the person

—Old Chinese Saying

CHAPTER FOCUS

You will begin learning about China's people and their lifestyles by reading about some Chinese people who have moved to Canada. As you read, think about the changes people might have to make when they move to a new country, and how these changes might affect their traditions and lifestyles. Try to answer the following questions:

- Why have some people moved from China to Canada?

- What are some changes Chinese people might make to live in Canada?

- How might the changes Chinese immigrants make affect their lifestyles and traditional beliefs?

RESEARCH

1. What do you know about your family's roots? Find out which countries your family originally came from. See if you can locate them on a map.

2. Talk to some of the older people in your family or community about why they or their ancestors came to Canada. Find out what experiences they had when they left their home countries for Canada. What changes did they have to make? Record this information in your notebook.

"When We Left China"

My name is Eileen Chu. I remember the day my family left for Canada. I had just had my ninth birthday. My mother woke me up at 6:30 AM to get ready for our big trip!

We had to go visit the graves of my grandmother and my great-grandparents. We had to say goodbye to them before we left China. Father said we needed to tell them where we were going so they could look after us in Canada.

After that, we had a big meal, with chicken, duck, fish, pork, and vegetables with rice. All our uncles, aunts, and cousins were there. I could not eat much because I was excited.

Then I changed into new clothes, a t-shirt and jeans. My grandfather had sent them to me from Canada. I remember they were too big!

Then it was time to leave. We had packed all our things a week before. We had many heavy suitcases and boxes.

"The bus stop was cluttered with suitcases, bicycles, knapsacks, and bags. While we waited for the bus to Guangzhou, we said goodbye to our family."

My uncles carried the suitcases and bags to the bus stop. We walked two blocks to where the small buses stopped. We were early and we waited. My father said we were going to Guangzhou to take the train to Hong Kong.

Then my sister started crying. My mother and my aunts cried too. I cried because I did not see my friends. They were in school.

At last the bus came. My second uncle helped us put the suitcases on the bus. There were not many seats left. I had to sit on my mother's lap all the way to Guangzhou. It was a long bus ride.

When we got to Guangzhou, it was very big and full of people and cars. My father got us a taxi to the train station. We took the train and stopped at Shenzhen. There, the guards checked our papers. They were friendly and wished us a good journey. Then we walked across to the Hong Kong side. Some more guards checked and stamped our passports. We then took the train all the way into Hong Kong. At the station, my mother's uncle met us. He took us to the airport in a taxi.

LET'S TALK ABOUT IT

1. In a group, discuss some reasons why people might move to a new country.

2. With your group, talk about how you would feel if you were moving to a new country.

READING MAPS

1. On a world map, locate China and Canada. Use the distance scale to find out how far Eileen had to travel when she left China and came to Canada. What ocean did she cross?

At the airport, there was a line-up, and we had to wait a long time. Then Great-Uncle took us to eat at a restaurant. But we did not have much time. The plane was leaving in an hour. We said goodbye at the gate. We all cried again. Then we got on the plane. It was a very big one, with rows of seats. We sat together in the middle. The flight attendants gave us lots of food. There was a movie, but I did not understand it because the actors spoke English.

I thought about my sister, my cousins, my uncles and aunts, and my friends. I did not know when I would see them again. Then I slept. My mother woke me up and told me we were arriving at Vancouver. It was early in the morning. We got off the plane and followed the people to **Customs**. We did not speak English and somebody came to help us.

The **translator** spoke Chinese, but a different kind of Chinese than we were used to. Finally, we were allowed to enter Canada. We got on another plane, this time to Edmonton.

On the way, we saw some snow-covered mountains. Then the land was flat, with many fields. I had never seen such big fields before. Then we had to fasten our seat belts. Soon we arrived in Edmonton. When we walked down the steps, my father shouted, "Father! Father!" He was calling to my grandfather, who was waiting for us at the airport. This was the first time I had met my grandfather. He was old and he had white hair. But he looked strong. He hugged my father, my brother, and picked me up and hugged me. Then he nodded to my mother. He took us to his car. It was a big, beautiful car! He drove us home. I had never seen such a beautiful home, with big gardens in the front and back. And such lovely flowers! Grandfather showed me to my own room! I was so tired that I slept until late the next day.

Eileen's Route from China to Canada

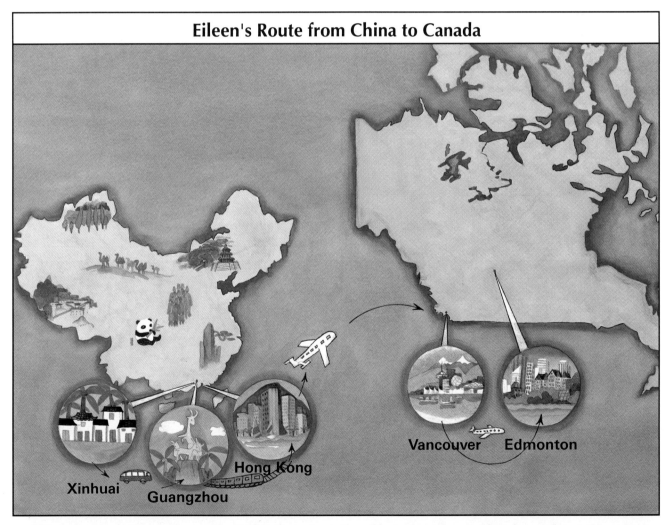

Xinhuai
Guangzhou
Hong Kong
Vancouver   Edmonton

"We took a bus to Guangzhou, and a taxi to the train station. The train took us to Shenzhen and on to Hong Kong. At Hong Kong, we went to the airport and flew to Vancouver, then on to Edmonton." Follow Eileen's route from Xinhuai, her home county in China, to her grandfather's home in Edmonton.

Why Eileen's Family Moved to Canada

Before Eileen and her family moved, her grandfather lived alone in Canada. After Eileen's grandmother died, her grandfather had moved to Canada because he did much business with Canadians. Although Grandfather made money in his business, he was lonely for his family. Because he was getting older, he needed his family's help. It is a Chinese tradition to honour and take care of family elders, so Eileen's father decided to move his family to Canada.

Eileen's family moved from their **ancestral village** of Zhonghao, in the county of Xinhuai. It was a long journey for the family, and a difficult move. It was hard to leave behind their many relatives and friends in China. Eileen's family moved to Canada to follow Chinese tradition, even though they had to make many changes in their lives.

When they moved to Canada, the Chu family had to learn a new language (English), make new friends, and get used to new foods, clothes, and homes. You will soon read about Eileen's first experiences in a Canadian school, where she had to learn many new ways as well as a new language.

An Important Tradition in Eileen's Family

It is an old tradition in China for people to keep ties with their ancestral villages. An ancestral village is the place where your ancestors were born. Eileen's ancestral village is where her great-grandmother, her grandfather, her father and she were all born.

Now that people in China are moving around more, some of the old ways are changing. Today people do not always live in their ancestral villages, but they still keep their ties with them.

Eileen's grandfather was the first one in the family to move to Canada. Eileen's family also left their ancestral village, but for all of them, Zhonghao was and always will be their ancestral home.

> ## LET'S TALK ABOUT IT
>
> 1. Imagine you are in a new country and do not speak the language. You are in the classroom for the first time. How would you like the other children to behave toward you? How should you behave toward your new classmates? Discuss your ideas in a small group, and share with your class.

Why would people leave their ancestral villages? What changes might they have to deal with?

"I Was Scared!"

A few days after we got to Canada, Grandfather said I must go to school. I was very scared. I did not know English and I had no friends. Grandfather, Father, and Mother came with me. We walked five blocks to a big, clean school. All the children were already in class. We went into the office and Grandfather talked to two women in English. One of the women wanted to shake my hand. I was afraid, so I did not look up.

The woman took my hand and walked me to a class-room. There were lots of boys and girls my age. Some were walking around the room, and some were talking! They were not at their desks and the teacher did not mind! The woman introduced me as Eileen. Grandfather whispered that from now on I would have an English name. He repeated it for me. Eileen. It sounded almost like my Chinese name, Ai-ling.

The teacher brought a girl to me whose name was Karen. I was happy she was Chinese. But I found out she could not speak Chinese! She said, ``Hi, Eileen!'' I did not say anything. I thought Canadian school was strange.

In China, we had to sit properly at our desks. We had to stand to greet our teachers when they came in. In Canada, children did not do that. Ms. Brown gave me a picture book to take home. I wanted to learn English quickly so that I could understand what people were saying.

Grandfather said if I studied hard, I could be a teacher like Ms. Brown. I had to help my parents learn English. They found it difficult. Sometimes they were not so happy. They had to work very hard. Even my brother said it was hard here. We missed all the people back in China. We did not yet have Canadian friends.

"I was surprised at how different school was in Canada. Grandfather, my teacher, and my new friends helped me get used to the new ways of doing things."

"Now I Feel At Home"

My father wants me to speak Chinese at home all the time. He sends me to Chinese school on Saturdays so I won't forget how to read and write Chinese. Sometimes I wish my parents would stop pushing so much Chinese. I wish they would call me Eileen rather than Ai-ling.

At first I missed my friends in China, but now I have lots of friends here. One day, when I grow up, I will visit all my cousins, uncles, and aunts, and my friends in China. I hope they will remember me!

THINK ABOUT IT

1. **In your notebook, describe the ways in which Eileen's lifestyle changed.**

2. **How have these changes affected her family?**

This woman lived in the city of Victoria in British Columbia in the early 1900s. Many Chinese people living in Canada at this time could not afford to send for their families in China to join them.

What Was It Like to Come to Canada One Hundred Years Ago?

Eileen and her family were not among the first people from China to move to Canada. In many ways, the challenges that the first **immigrants** from China faced were much tougher.

One hundred years ago, people who wanted to move to Canada from countries like England, Scotland, France, or Germany could simply come. However, there was a **Head Tax** for Chinese immigrants. This meant that Chinese people had to pay before they could enter Canada. At first, the tax was $50 per person. Then it rose to $100, and finally to $500. This was a tremendous sum of money at that time! Most Chinese workers could not earn enough to pay for whole families to come to Canada.

In 1923, the Head Tax was ended. But a new law allowed only certain people into Canada. This law kept most new Chinese immigrants out of Canada. It was not until 1947 that the law was changed, allowing more Chinese to come to Canada.

Sam Li's Story

In 1858, I was among the first Chinese who came to Canada. We came by boat and arrived at the Pacific port of Victoria, British Columbia. Some of my family came from San Francisco, in California, to join the rush for gold!

*We were looking for better opportunities in this new land. In China, at this time, people were starving to death because of **famine** and poverty.*

More Chinese workers continued to come. In the 1880s, Canada was building a railway from the Atlantic to the Pacific. Canada did not have enough people to build it quickly. Many Chinese people came from the United States and from China to work on the railway.

In many ways, I felt that we were welcomed only because we were able to help build the railway. We were paid less than the other workers. Yet, many Canadians were upset that the railway jobs went to the Chinese.

Working on the railway was hard. Many of my friends died from the work, and were buried by the tracks.

*When the railway was finished, Canadian **authorities** made it difficult for some of us to remain in Canada. Some of my friends sailed back home. Others, like myself, stayed in Canada and made it our home.*

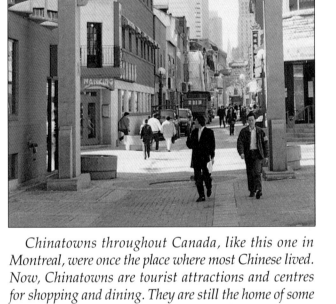

Chinatowns throughout Canada, like this one in Montreal, were once the place where most Chinese lived. Now, Chinatowns are tourist attractions and centres for shopping and dining. They are still the home of some Chinese elders and new immigrants.

Where Did Early Chinese Immigrants Settle in Canada?

Few of the early Chinese immigrants spoke English, or understood the customs of their new country. Because the Chinese could not communicate in English, and because they dressed differently and ate different foods, they were treated differently.

They were not welcomed by some Canadians and were forbidden to do many things. They lived in certain parts of the cities and formed their own neighbourhoods. Their neighbourhoods became known as Chinatowns.

The first and largest of the Chinatowns was located in Victoria, British Columbia. Victoria was the port of entry for most Chinese into Canada, whether they came from China or from the United States.

Other Chinatowns sprang up in cities such as Vancouver, Calgary, Edmonton, Ottawa, Toronto, Winnipeg, and Montreal. Chinese immigrants followed the railway that they had helped to build, and settled in towns throughout Canada.

Today, not all Chinese in Canada live in Chinatowns. Eileen Chu is a good example. Families, like Eileen's, that move to Canada from China now live in every part of the country.

A LOOK BACK

This chapter focussed on Chinese people who have moved to Canada. Some Chinese, like Eileen Chu's family, moved to Canada to keep their traditional ways. Others, like Sam Li, came to Canada because it offered more opportunities for a better way of life.

When people move to a new country, they often need to make changes in their lifestyles. The Chinese people had to learn a new language, English, and had to get used to new foods, homes, transportation, and customs. The stories in this chapter helped to show how change can be difficult, especially when a person must leave behind friends, family members, and the customs they are comfortable with. These stories also described how Canadians can help immigrants feel at home in their new country. Through the stories of Eileen Chu and Sam Li, we have learned that building relationships with people in a new country is very important. It is also important for Chinese people to maintain their relationships with family and friends in China, because of traditional links to ancestral villages and the importance of family ties.

Moving to a new country creates change in people's lives. The need to keep traditions can create change. The need to develop relationships with others can also create conflict. In Eileen Chu's family, Eileen's need to make new friends and speak English has caused some conflict with her parents, who want her to keep her traditional language. As Eileen lives longer in Canada, other changes may occur. All the changes which take place in her life, however, will be influenced by traditional Chinese beliefs and customs.

As Eileen shares some of these traditions with her new Canadian friends, their lives will also change. Just as the Chinatowns of today offer visitors the chance to experience Chinese customs, Eileen's relationship with her new friends will teach them more about China.

A LOOK AHEAD

- Just as Eileen's relationship with other Canadians has grown, relationships between countries have changed and developed. You will soon read about the growing relationship between Canada and other Pacific Rim countries.
- Countries whose borders are close to other countries are called neighbours. Pacific Rim countries all share a border on the Pacific Ocean. They consider the Pacific Rim to be an important neighbourhood.
- China is one of Canada's Pacific Rim neighbours.
- Countries on the Pacific Rim share their goods, services, ideas, and lifestyles in many ways.
- The ways in which Pacific Rim countries act towards each other is becoming more important to Canada and China.

Questions

1. Turn back to the Chapter Focus questions on page 1. Answer these questions in your notebook. Discuss your answers with a partner.

2. Sam Li's story described work on a Canadian railway in the 1800s. Even though the work was hard and dangerous, many Chinese men came to Canada to do the job. What needs were they meeting by doing so?

3. What aspects of Chinese lifestyles do you think Chinatowns share with the people who visit them? Why do you think Chinatowns are important to many Chinese Canadians?

4. Eileen's family and Sam Li had very different experiences in Canada. Why do you think this is so? (Hint: Think about what might have changed in China and Canada in the past one hundred years.)

5. Compare the experiences of Eileen Chu and Sam Li. Make a chart to show the things which made their moves to Canada easier, and which made the moves more difficult. What do their stories tell you about change and its effect on people's lifestyles? Record your thoughts on change below your chart.

Activities

1. Draw a picture which shows some details of Eileen's journey to Canada. Below the picture, write a few sentences describing what Eileen is experiencing in the picture.

2. Collect several pictures and words from magazines and newspapers to tell the story of Eileen's and Sam's experiences as new citizens of Canada. Attach these pictures to story cards and share your story with a group.

CHAPTER 2

Many Neighbours on the Pacific Rim

Crows are black

All over the world

—Old Chinese Saying

CHAPTER FOCUS

You will read about the countries of the Pacific Rim and why they are becoming more important to Canada. Think about the ways in which Canada shares things with other countries on the Pacific Rim. Think also about how the sharing between Canada and China might affect the lives of Canadian and Chinese people. Try to answer the following questions:

• Why is the Pacific Rim becoming more important?

• What kinds of relationships have developed between Canada and other Pacific Rim countries?

• What are some examples of sharing among Pacific Rim countries?

• Why do Pacific Rim countries share with each other?

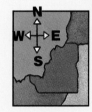

READING MAPS

1. **Look at the map on the next page. Identify the countries on the Pacific Rim. List them in two columns, east side and west side of the Pacific Rim.**

2. **Why do you think countries on the Pacific Rim began to think of one another as neighbours?**

3. **On a world map, use the latitude and longitude grid system to locate Canada and China.**

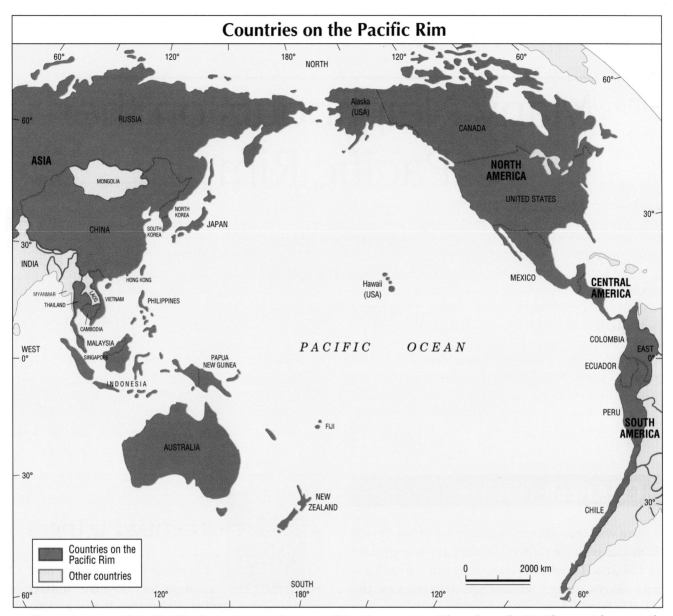

Countries on the Pacific Rim

Countries around the Pacific Ocean have at least one thing in common. They share the Pacific coast from north to south and east to west. They are Pacific Rim neighbours.

What Is the Pacific Rim?

The Pacific Ocean is the largest ocean in the world. Its size once made it difficult for the people who lived in countries around the Pacific Ocean to communicate with each other.

Today, jet planes, faster ships, facsimile machines and telephones have made the Pacific seem smaller. These modern technologies have helped the peoples who live around this ocean become trading partners.

Many countries border the Pacific Ocean. In all, the Pacific Rim stretches from Chile in South America, to Alaska in the Arctic. On the other side of the Pacific Ocean, it stretches from New Zealand to Russia.

In Canada, the term "Pacific Rim neighbours" usually refers to our neighbours in Asia. These neighbours extend from Japan and Korea in the north, to Indonesia in the south. For Canada, the idea of trading with Pacific Rim neighbours became more popular as communication and transportation across the Pacific Ocean improved. Now the Pacific Rim countries in Asia have replaced Europe as Canada's main trading partners, after the United States.

Why Is the Pacific Rim Becoming More Important?

There are several reasons why the Pacific Rim is becoming more important. The nations of the Pacific Rim form the *largest* market in the world. Billions of people live in the Pacific Rim countries. They make and buy many products. Some of the countries have abundant natural resources, such as energy and minerals. Pacific Rim countries are also major food-producing nations.

Pacific Rim trade is growing, and tourism is also on the increase. Pacific Rim neighbours share special projects with each other, and in some cases, schools, towns, cities, and provinces are **twinned**. For example, China's Heilongjiang province is twinned with Alberta. This sharing helps build strong bonds between the people of one Pacific Rim nation and another.

As you read on, you will learn more about Pacific Rim trade, tourism, and twinning.

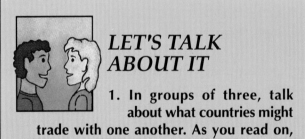

LET'S TALK ABOUT IT

1. In groups of three, talk about what countries might trade with one another. As you read on, compare your predictions with the facts.

SHARING

1. Give one example of how China's Heilongjiang and Canada's Alberta share. State how Canadian and Chinese people could share with each other. You may want to continue reading this chapter before you answer this question.

People are one of the most important resources along the Pacific Rim.

Canada's Trading Partners on the Pacific Rim

Since the 1960s, countries on the Asian side of the Pacific Rim have greatly increased their production of goods. One such country is Japan. By the late 1970s, Japan was one of Canada's most important trading partners.

In the 1990s, Canada's trade grew rapidly with other Asian Pacific Rim partners, such as Singapore, Taiwan, Hong Kong, and South Korea. Because of their ability to produce many goods for trading, these countries are called "the Four Tigers."

Trade between Canada and China is increasing, and the countries are exchanging a greater variety of goods. This relationship is not new. For many years, merchants from both countries have been crossing the Pacific to trade. One of the first products ever traded was ginseng, a root which has medicinal qualities. Another popular trade item was, and still is, tea.

People throughout the world drink tea every day. Some of it will have been packed by tea factory workers like Li Weiyong.

A Friendly Cup of Tea

Both Canadians and Chinese use tea. Much of the tea we drink in Canada comes from China. In fact, it is thought that Marco Polo, an explorer from Italy, "discovered" tea on his trip to China.

Tea is sold in little bags or loose in tins or boxes. Millions of people throughout the world drink it every day. Li Weiyong is a worker in a tea factory in Fushan, Fujian province. She tells how tea has affected her life:

I have been working in this factory since I left elementary school. My family lived in the country. My parents had a big family, so I had to work.

I first started as a tea leaf sorter. My job was to sort the type and size of tea leaves after the pickers brought them in from the fields. Then the leaves were laid out on huge bamboo trays to dry. After they were dry, the leaves were packed.

I am now a tea packer. I pack tea into large tins or into individual paper bags for the food stores. The more expensive teas are packed in tins to keep them fresh longer. I also pack tea into pretty boxes for **export***.*

Trade between China and Canada has changed the way Canadians and Chinese live. Canadians wear clothing made of silk and cotton made in China. Chinese eat noodles made with Canadian wheat. A Chinese friend may call a Canadian friend on the telephone. The telephone was designed in Canada, but made in China.

Canada sells a great amount of wheat to China. Canadians are also interested in selling other things to the Chinese. Canadian companies making oil drilling equipment, satellite dishes, airplanes, and mining machinery, all sell some of their products in China. They, and other Canadian businesses, would like to sell more products to China in the future.

Air China brings Chinese tourists to Canada and Canadian tourists to China.

Links Between People on the Pacific Rim

Tourism between countries on the Pacific Rim has increased. By 1990, over 950 000 tourists a year were visiting Canada from Asian countries bordering the Pacific. More Canadians are also visiting Asia.

The number of immigrants from the Pacific Rim to Canada has also increased. In 1990, over 50 per cent of new immigrants to Canada came from Asian countries on the Pacific Rim.

In order to trade more and to know more about each other, Canada and China established **diplomatic relations** in October, 1970. China opened an embassy in Ottawa, and Canada opened an embassy in Beijing. This made it easier for people to visit one another's country. As you will see, however, not *all* tourists are *people*!

Inez Morris was one of the Canadians who went to China to bring two giant pandas back to Canada for the Calgary Olympics in 1988.

As you read Inez's account of her tour of China, find each of the places she mentions on the map. Trace her trip. Where did her group go to get the pandas?

Two Special Tourists from China

In 1988, I went to China with a group of people who worked for the Calgary Zoo. We went there to bring two giant pandas back to Canada. While in China we saw many beautiful sights.

Our plane landed in Hong Kong. We took a train from Hong Kong into China. We traveled past rice fields. Everywhere we looked, men and women were running in rapid, sure steps over the ridges between fields. Or they were hauling produce, soil, or rocks in buckets hanging from each end of a bamboo rod slung across their shoulders. Water buffalo were used to carry things, too. Everyone was working hard!

We also took a four hour cruise on the Lijiang. The river was dotted with bamboo rafts and people who were fishing by using cormorants. A cormorant is a large sea bird with webbed feet. It is an excellent fish catcher. It can catch as many fish in one hour as three people! This bird has a long, hooked bill and a brightly coloured pouch of skin under its mouth. People have the birds on a leash so they can take the fish that the bird catches.

Guilin has some of the most beautiful scenery in the world. Like Inez, many people take short cruises along the Lijiang to admire the view.

The giant panda is one of the rarest animals in the world. People from many countries are working to help China save the giant panda.

During the cruise, we could see the hills of Guilin in the distance. Han Yu, a writer who lived during the T'ang Dynasty, once wrote about this area, "the river is a blue silk ribbon and the hills are jade hairpins."

Another day, we took a bus to the Wolong Reserve. On the way, we traveled through the "food basket of China." Every bit of land was carefully farmed or gardened. As the bus climbed into the hills, we could see that the farmers' struggle for survival meant that they had to cut down the bamboo forests.

I thought about how pandas need the bamboo forests to survive. Forests all over the world are in danger. In China, forests are disappearing at a rate of 2.5 hectares every minute. The loss of the forests is creating many problems. The soil is eroding, and grassland is turning into desert. Pandas are losing the places where they live in the wild.

Our tour included a trip to the Great Wall, 40 km from Beijing. Finally, we went to Beijing, the capital city of China, to pick up the giant pandas. The pandas had been shipped to Beijing by train.

The two pandas were named Xi Xi and Qun Qun. We put them on a Canadian Airlines plane named the Panda Special. It was a special plane, all right.

Eight seats on the plane were removed to accommodate the cages carrying the two 110 kg giant pandas. Xi Xi and Qun Qun were two very special tourists. They rode first class all the way!

Some of us heard a soft yip from Xi Xi when we took off. The Chinese veterinarian and our own zoo veterinarian watched for any problems, but the pandas seemed to be looking forward to their adventure. Apples and lots of fresh, sweet-smelling bamboo were stored near the cages. Since a panda eats for about 14 hours each day, most of the food had disappeared by the time we landed in Canada.

The Calgary Zoo was ready to welcome the pandas. While at the zoo, Xi Xi and Qun Qun ate a gruel made from soya powder, ground carrots, milk and brown rice powder. Their main food was bamboo grown especially for them in the zoo conservatory. Bamboo was also imported weekly from San Diego, California.

The pandas stayed seven months in Canada. They were admired by over 1 million visitors to the zoo.

Some zoologists believe that pandas are bears. Others believe that pandas are more closely related to the raccoon family. However, there is no disagreement about the danger facing pandas. The giant panda is on the **endangered species** list. In 1990, there were only 1000 giant pandas alive in the world.

THINK ABOUT IT

1. **When people think of animals from China, they think of giant pandas.**
   (a) **Which animals are associated with Canada?**
   (b) **Where do these animals live in Canada?**
   (c) **Are they endangered?**

2. **How might the visit of two giant pandas from China at the Calgary Zoo have made the relationship between Canada and China stronger?**

Twinning Between Pacific Rim Neighbours

Many Canadian towns, cities, and provinces have set up ties with Pacific Rim countries. They call each other *twins*. Even schools have twinned with other schools on the Pacific Rim. People twin so that they can get to know each other better.

Groups like the Canada-China Friendship Association organize twinning between Canada and China. Twinning can also be organized by governments. Twinning encourages people from both countries to learn more about each other's culture and history. For example, the Association organizes information evenings to teach the twins about each other. These evenings often include slide shows, dinners, and speakers. The Association also sets up tours for groups such as artists, athletes, students, doctors, and teachers from one twin to visit similar groups in the other twin city or province.

Edmonton is twinned with Harbin in China. Toronto's twin is Chongqing and Calgary's is Daqing.

Alberta's twin province is Heilongjiang. Saskatchewan is twinned with Jilin, and Ontario with Jiangsu. Canada also twins with other countries on the Pacific Rim. For example, Jasper, Alberta is twinned with the mountain resort city of Hakone in Japan.

Twinning has helped many Canadian and Chinese students learn more about each other's countries. Hundreds of Canadian students have traveled to China. There, they visited their provinces' twins, attended Chinese schools, met Chinese students, and saw sights they had only read about before! Many Chinese youngsters have made similar trips to their Canadian twins.

THE DINOSAUR PROJECT

Many years ago, an adventurer named Roy Chapman Andrews, from Indiana in the United States, made some exciting discoveries in China. You may not have heard of him, but you probably have heard of a movie character named Indiana Jones. Indiana Jones is based on the real-life Roy Chapman Andrews!

A Canadian scientist, Phil Currie, was inspired by Andrews to lead the first **palaeontological** expedition to China's Gobi Desert in 60 years. Dr. Currie is the head of Alberta's Royal Tyrrell Museum of Palaeontology, in Drumheller.

Together with colleagues from Canada and China, Dr. Currie has helped organize several expeditions, in the Gobi and in Alberta's badlands. Both areas are rich in dinosaur bones. Many of the dinosaur bones that the scientists discover will be put together into a display. The display will be called the Dinosaur Project, and it will be the largest traveling show about dinosaurs ever held. It will tour the world in the 1990s.

Several groups are working on the Dinosaur Project. Together, they are called the EX TERRA Foundation. They are based in Edmonton, Alberta.

EX TERRA includes the National Museum of Canada, the Royal Tyrrell Museum of Palaeontology, the Chinese Academy of Sciences, and the governments of Canada, China, and Alberta.

SHARING

1. **Canada and China share information through the Dinosaur Project. Record your ideas about how sharing this project might help each country.**

A LOOK BACK

The ways in which the Pacific Rim countries relate to one another is changing. As modern technologies made it easier for people in these countries to communicate with others, the relationship grew stronger. People in Pacific Rim countries found that trading with each other would benefit them all.

As the relationship among Pacific Rim countries developed, Canada and China became more important to each other. Both countries had products that could be used by the other, and a trading relationship grew. The need to have products which improve people's lifestyles was, therefore, met by this trading relationship.

The relationship between Canada and China has expanded to include shared projects like the Dinosaur Project, increased tourism between countries, and twinning of schools, towns, cities, and provinces. This growing relationship between Canada's and China's peoples helps meet the need to learn more about lifestyles in each other's countries. As in our relationships with other people, the more countries know about one another, the stronger the relationship will be.

Sharing between Canada and China has benefited the people in both countries and has made their relationship more important than ever before.

A LOOK AHEAD

- As relationships change, we want to get to know others better. The next chapter will tell you about China's past.

- China's past influences the way people think and behave today.

- Chinese beliefs began long ago.

- Students in China have tried to change some traditional Chinese beliefs.

- Some Chinese felt the need to change as China became more involved with other countries.

- China's physical size and large population often made change slow and difficult.

Questions

1. Turn back to the Chapter Focus questions on page 9. Answer these questions in your notebook. Discuss your answers with a classmate.

2. What things do Canada and China share? List the examples described in this chapter. Beside each example, explain how the sharing might affect the ways in which Canadian and Chinese people meet their needs.

3. What products does Canada trade with the other Pacific Rim countries? Identify three things in your home that came from a Pacific Rim country.

4. China's foresters have cut down much of China's forests to make trees into wood products, and to free land for fields. More fields can grow more food for more people. Is something similar happening in Canada? Why? Do we need to cut down our forests? What choices do Canadians have?

5. Do you think that the relationship among Pacific Rim countries is important? Tell why in two or three sentences.

Activities

1. The panda is an endangered animal in China. There are also endangered animals in Canada. Find out which animals are endangered in Canada and what is being done to protect these animals from extinction. Write a report which records your findings. Include pictures or drawings of the animals and a map which shows the original habitats of these animals.

2. On page viii of this text, there is a map of the world. On page 10, there is another map of the world. These maps have some differences. Both, however, feature the Pacific Ocean at their centres. What world view do these maps convey? What are some other ways of showing the world? Look in an atlas and find another type of world map. Write a brief report listing the differences between it and the maps on pages viii and 10.

CHAPTER 3

China's Past—Its Ties to Today

Ice three feet thick is not frozen in a day

◊

If you wish to succeed

Consult three old people

—Old Chinese Saying

CHAPTER FOCUS

You have learned some things about the changing relationship between China and Canada. One part of relationships is to get to know each other better. Learning about China's past will help you understand China's people today.

You will read about governments and ideas from China's past that helped the Chinese meet their need to live in harmony with others. You will also read about how and why the Chinese changed their governments and ideas over time. As you read, think about whether or not these changes would help the Chinese to live in social harmony with people in other parts of the world. Try to answer these questions:

- What did the Chinese believe in in the past?

- How have Chinese beliefs changed over time?

- What happened to change the way the Chinese looked at other nations in the world?

- How have the changes helped China live in harmony with other countries?

THINK ABOUT IT

1. Humans have many different kinds of needs. One of these is "the need to know." We want to understand our world, ourselves, and our history. In your notebook, write five important events from your personal history. How have these events affected your family?

2. Record five events in Canada's history and describe how these events affected Canadians and the ways they live.

Discovering the Past

Archeologists have long believed that Chinese civilization began in the Wei River valley, near present-day Xi'an, in the bend of the Huang (*Yellow*) he (*River*). Early villages have been **excavated** and evidence of early life, in the form of pottery, has been found. The differences in the pottery samples found suggests that villages had special styles of pottery. For example, some pottery had a rope design, while other pottery was shiny and black.

Archeologists continue to search for clues to China's past. Recent evidence suggests that China may have had its beginnings in other places, too.

READING MAPS

1. Archeologists search areas such as river valleys, because these places are suitable for human settlement, in terms of climate, raw materials, and fertile soil or animals for food. Pretend you are an archeologist. On a map of China, point out where you would look for evidence of the first Chinese villages.

The Wei River Valley

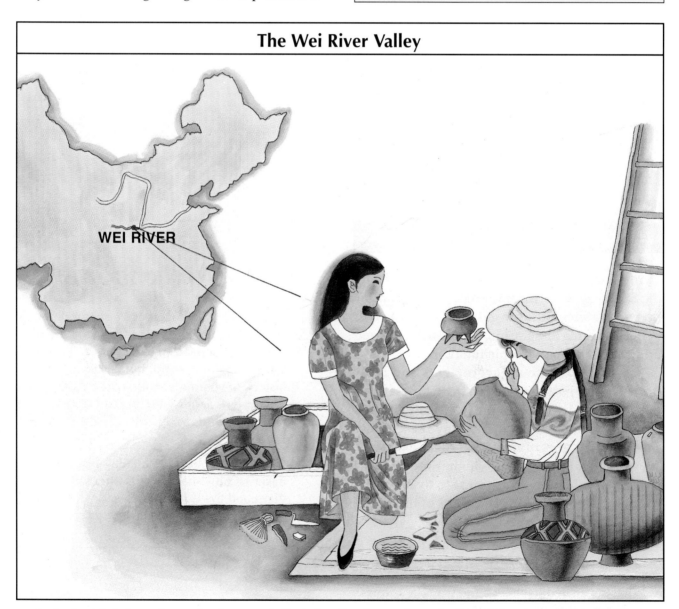

WEI RIVER

Archeologists help us learn about our past. Studying the places where the first Chinese people lived helps us to know what kind of lives they led. What do you think archeologists can tell by looking at old pottery found in early Chinese villages?

IMPORTANT DATES

China's history stretches far back into the past. Many important events have taken place over the centuries. Refer to these dates whenever you want to remind yourself of China's early history.

500 000 BC The time of the **Peking Man**, an early ancestor of present-day Chinese.

1650-1027 BC The time of the Shang **Dynasty**, one of the earliest dynasties in China. During this dynasty, an alphabet was used. The writing was done on bones and tortoise shells.

1027-256 BC The time of the Zhou Dynasty. China's major **philosophers**, Confucius and Laozi, lived during this time. Also, the compass was invented.

221 BC Emperor Qin Shi Huangdi unified China as a country. The Great Wall of China was begun during this time. A system of weights and measures was also adopted, and a common method of writing was developed.

206 BC-220 AD The time of the Han Dynasty. This dynasty gave the majority of Chinese their name: the Han. During this time, China made its first contacts with Europe (the Roman Empire). China also invented paper-making and the **seismograph**. Buddhism came from India to China at this time.

800 AD Gunpowder was invented. This was 300 years before it was used in Europe.

1271-1295 Marco Polo traveled in China.

1610 The first Jesuit mission in China was begun by Matteo Ricci, a missionary. The Jesuits remained in China as missionaries until 1722.

1644-1912 The time of the Qing Dynasty. This was the last of China's dynasties.

RESEARCH

1. Look in an encyclopedia to find out more about one dynasty. Why was this dynasty important to China's history?

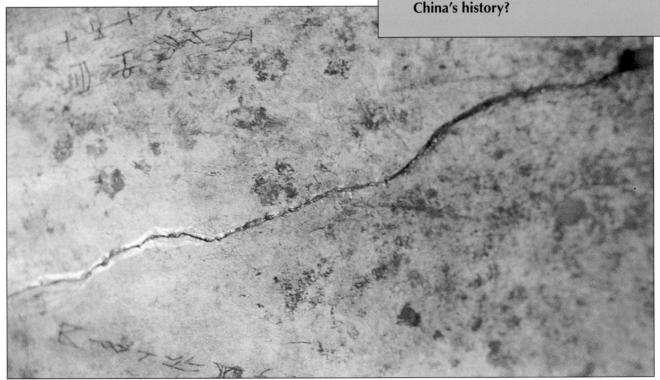

Early Chinese had a need to write things down. During the Shang Dynasty, writing was done on bones and tortoise shells. This example of bone writing is over 2000 years old.

Chinese Dynasties

For over 2000 years, China had a government based on the rule of dynasties. A dynasty was created when a series of emperors came from the same family. Led by emperors, China's dynasties provided order and stability, two important needs in a big country with a large population.

The royal family set rules for who would hold power. Usually, a dying emperor would say which of his sons would rule after him. The great Chinese dynasties sometimes lasted for several centuries. One emperor would **succeed** another in regular fashion. A dynasty would continue until it was defeated by a different family.

One of the earliest dynasties emerged in north China: the Shang Dynasty. This dynasty was made up of the Shang family.

During the Shang Dynasty, many Chinese believed there were two worlds—a spirit world and a human world. One of the Shang emperors' jobs was to serve as a link between these two worlds. People believed that if a Shang emperor ruled badly, he would be punished by the spirits!

After many centuries, the Shang Dynasty was replaced by a powerful family called the Zhou. In time, however, the Zhou rulers lost much of their authority. The Zhou empire gradually broke up into **city-states** that were at war with one another.

Battle of Ideas

While the leaders of these warring states fought each other with arrows and swords, their philosophers carried out a battle of ideas. It was a time of great uncertainty. Great thinkers, such as Confucius and Laozi, searched for the best way to organize society and government. Both Confucius and Laozi created rules that helped provide peace, **harmony**, and **prosperity** for their followers.

MINI STUDY: *The Confucian Order*

As you read this Mini Study, think of why Confucianism became the most popular set of beliefs in China.

The ancient Chinese looked for the best ways to maintain order and harmony among people. They found this system in the writings of a man named Confucius. He lived from 551 to 478 BC.

Confucius taught people how they should behave. He taught that people should cooperate and not harm anything or one another.

Confucius believed that if everyone in society knew his or her place, and followed the rules, then society would be in harmony.

To Confucius, the most important group in society was the scholars, followed by farmers, because they produced food. Artists came next because they produced things. Merchants were at the bottom because they produced nothing and took wealth from people. They were not respected and were harshly **regulated** by the government.

Confucius explained the proper relationship of husband to wife, father to son, mother to daughter, elder brother to younger brother, friend to friend, and ruler to subject. He based his ideas on the family. When people knew their place and how to behave in the family and in society, they could live in harmony. The need for harmony is important to the Chinese, now and in the past.

According to this set of beliefs, the emperor was the most powerful person on Earth. He could bring harmony between the government and the people, with the blessing of heaven. This Confucian belief touched every level of life in China. Young, old, rich, poor, rulers, and common people were all supposed to follow the Confucian order. Even to this day, we can see the important influence of the Confucian order on the way Chinese people behave toward each other.

Questions

1. Confucius wrote about special ways that people should relate to one another. Sit together in groups of three and talk about how you relate to others in your family. Ask one another these questions:

(a) In your family, are there special ways that you relate to the adults?

(b) Is this different from the way you relate to your brothers or sisters?

(c) Do you treat your parents the same way you treat your teacher?

The Influence of the Han Dynasty

After a long period of fighting, Qin Shi Huangdi emerged as China's emperor. His rule was followed by the Han Dynasty, which ruled from 206 BC to 220 AD. The Han people are still the most **dominant** people in China today. It was the Han Dynasty that adopted Confucianism as the philosophy to guide society and government. As a result, the Confucian way of doing things was kept in place in China for more than 2000 years, until 1912.

China: The Middle Kingdom

The Chinese were proud and confident of themselves. For many centuries, they thought their history, customs, ideas, and lifestyle were better than anyone else's. They thought of China as the centre of the world, and called their country "Middle Kingdom," or Zhongguo in Chinese. It seemed only natural to the Chinese that the less cultured people of the world would like to learn from China.

The Chinese were correct in much of their belief. China was famous in many parts of the world by the 1500s. Visitors marveled at the quality of life the Chinese had and at the wonderful art forms the Chinese created. Over the centuries, the Chinese way of life had become very **sophisticated**. Early explorers from Europe, such as Marco Polo, were impressed by it.

The Chinese made many discoveries and invented many things, like gunpowder and silk, long before these things were known elsewhere in the world.

The Chinese believed that their greatest strength was their superior way of life. They did not really need powerful armies to control their borders. They believed their way of life would keep would-be invaders away. After all, who would dare invade the centre of the world?!

SOLDIERS OF CLAY

In 1974, some Chinese farmers decided to dig a new well. Instead of water, they discovered some life-sized clay men and horses!

Archeologists were called to the site. They discovered hundreds of men—in fact, they uncovered a whole army—complete with armour, weapons, and horses. The men were made of terra cotta, or clay.

In 221 BC, Emperor Qin Shi Huangdi ordered sculptors to make models of his army of soldiers. He ordered that they be buried near his tomb outside the city of Xi'an. Over the years, the clay army was forgotten. In fact, it was forgotten for 2000 years.

Now, people may visit this amazing army, which still stands guard at the emperor's tomb.

Millions of tourists have seen the amazing terra cotta army near Xi'an.

Why Were Foreigners Interested in China?

Many countries were very eager to trade with China. And by the early 1800s, many European nations and the United States began to do so.

The Chinese thought it was only natural that foreigners would want to come to China. They believed foreign people would want to learn from the emperor. They also believed these people would want to enjoy the benefits of the Chinese way of life.

Because so many foreigners wished to come to China, the Chinese decided to regulate their visits. Some were allowed to come every year, like the Koreans. Some were allowed to come every few years, like the Vietnamese, Japanese, and Burmese.

Many Chinese thought that people were coming to learn from them. However, most foreigners were seldom interested in becoming like the Chinese. They came to trade and to make **profits**.

In 1839, the British sent warships to China and forced the emperor to allow traders into the country. China was forced to open its doors to the rest of the world.

The British tried to control trade by selling **opium** to the Chinese. The British brought the opium from India to exchange for Chinese products. The Chinese were against the opium trade

Foreigners marveled at the inventions and art forms that the Chinese worked with. A device for charting the stars, like this one, was made by the Chinese together with Western missionaries.

and tried to fight off the British. The wars that resulted weakened the emperor and his dynasty. By 1911-1912, the Chinese empire had collapsed.

Confucianism, the philosophy that had served China so well for centuries, was now discredited. Chinese scholars and students began to look to **Western ideas**. Western science and ways of life were valued by many students, who tried to learn new ways of doing things to help build a new China.

Why Did the Dynasties End?

The traditional government of China was made up of dynasties. The emperors who ruled kept the power of government within their own families. Why did a system that had worked for thousands of years end?

In the old system of dynasties, the emperors were expected to provide a good example for the people to follow, and to punish most severely those who failed to follow that example. Everyone knew his or her place and acted accordingly. The traditional system had almost no elements like our government within it. For example, there were no elections and there were no political parties.

In the 1800s, however, European countries began to spread their influence around the world. A number of Chinese students and government officials began to want to have a Western style of government. The students and officials thought the traditional system had failed. This was the beginning of the push to end the dynasties.

The Chinese government fought against the opium trade in China. This picture shows soldiers burning boxes of opium.

Dr. Sun and Change

One person who was very concerned with the weak condition of China was a Chinese doctor named Sun Yat-sen. Dr. Sun was a rebel against the emperor's government. He was forced to spend much of his time between 1895 and 1911 away from China.

Dr. Sun wanted to change the government in China. He developed ideas that would make China a **republic**. This new China would be more like Western countries.

Dr. Sun raised money from Chinese who had settled overseas to assist him in bringing down the weakened emperor.

He visited Canada three times and raised money to support **revolts** against the government in China. In 1911, one of the revolts succeeded. Dr. Sun now had an opportunity to establish a new government in China.

Unfortunately for Dr. Sun, he had not lived in China long enough to have a large following of people who agreed with him. He was defeated by warlords, leaders who controlled large private armies.

Warlords destroyed what was left of the old empire. During this time, the Chinese people suffered. Their farms were not producing enough food. With foreigners invading their land and the warlords destroying their lives, the people had little hope for the future.

RESEARCH

1. Why did Dr. Sun Yat-sen want to change China?

2. What were some of his ideas? Record your answers in your notebook.

Warlords took control of China when it was in a weakened state. They made the country even weaker.

Students Support Change

China's university students looked for ways to change their country. They studied American and Russian ways of life, including forms of government. The students began to organize themselves into groups to make changes. They wanted to change China, to reflect their new political ideas.

In the end, two new Chinese political parties were formed. One, called the Nationalists (Guomindang), was led first by Sun Yat-sen. Later Chiang K'ai-shek became its leader. This party ruled China from 1927 to 1949. After a bitter civil war, the other party, the **Communists** (Gongchandang), led by Mao Zedong, defeated the Nationalists in 1949 and established the People's Republic of China.

Dr. Sun Yat-sen lived much of his life outside of China. He was interested in new ways of doing things and brought new ideas back to China. He wanted to change China.

Why Did China Change Its Ways?

Looking inward had kept China from knowing what was going on around the world. The Chinese need for harmony, to live in peace, prompted them to build the Great Wall hundreds of years ago to keep out foreign invaders. They developed great traditions and inventions which were admired by foreigners. They felt proud of themselves and were content to be the "centre of the world." Because their country was so large and its **economy** was rich and diverse, they had no need to trade with foreigners.

Because China was isolated from the rest of the world by its belief in its superior way of life, China became weaker. It fell behind other countries which shared new ideas with one another through trade.

China was weakened to the point where it could not defend itself from foreign invasion. Eventually, China was forced to open its doors to foreign powers. It needed to re-examine its position in the world. China realized that it must **modernize** in order to survive as a country. It was the students who helped to push for modernization. Even today, Chinese students play an important role in helping China to become modern.

The Great Wall was built by joining together many shorter walls. It was built to protect China from northern invaders.

A LOOK BACK

Beliefs, systems of government, and events helped shape China's history. Just as things in your life help to determine the kind of person you are, countries also develop according to influences and events in their past. China's past has, therefore, influenced the way China is today.

Archeologists have found that early ancestors of the Chinese lived as long ago as 500 000 BC. The evidence found by archeologists helps us understand how early Chinese met their needs. Remember, many of the earliest settlements were in river valleys because these areas provided the basic essentials for meeting needs of food, clothing, and shelter.

From village settlements China developed into a much larger territory. Powerful families took control of this area and provided the necessary order and stability for China's growing population. You have learned that these powerful families ruled for long periods of time and that each of these periods was called a dynasty. Dynasties governed China for over 2000 years.

Change in China was a slow process. The large area and population of China, coupled with the Chinese belief that their way of living was superior to those of other peoples, meant that China did not develop strong relationships with other countries. When China could no longer keep other countries from entering and trading with its merchants, traditional dynasty rule ended.

China's period of dynasty rule ended because it could not meet the Chinese people's need for new knowledge and products. Several Chinese people, among them Dr. Sun Yat-sen, Chiang K'ai-shek, and Mao Zedong, questioned the traditional ideas of Confucianism and worked to change China's government. Students in China supported these changes and, as you will read later, still work for change.

China's past shows that change takes place when the needs of a country's population are not being met. China's isolation from other countries made it harder for China to "catch up" to other nations who had shared ideas through trade. China's long history also meant that traditional ways of doing things were long established. Because traditions are important to the people who practise them, it is difficult to change quickly.

In future chapters, you will read about ways in which China is changing. As you read, think about China's long history. It will help you to understand how change in China can be a difficult process. It will also help you to understand how the Chinese people's pride in their country and their abilities help them to meet the need for change.

A LOOK AHEAD

- Just as a people's history affects the way they live, so does the geography of the place they live in.
- China is one of the world's largest countries. Its landscape is varied, and China is home to many different peoples.
- China's climate is quite different from Canada's and greatly affects the way the Chinese people live.
- China's landscape and climate also affect where the people live.
- With such a large country, and so many people living in it, communication is an interesting problem for China.

Questions

1. Look back at the Chapter Focus questions. Record your answers in your notebook. Record one fact about China's past that interested you the most and explain why it interested you.
2. For many years, the Chinese thought of China as the Middle Kingdom. They did not care to have relationships with other countries. How did this benefit the Chinese people? How did it cause difficulty for them?
3. What need was being met when China began to modernize, or use ideas from other countries? What effect did this have on the traditional ways of doing things?

Activities

1. Create a timeline of the events in China's history which you have read about in this chapter. Use drawings to make your timeline more interesting.
2. Select one person, event, or dynasty in China's past that interests you. Research your topic using several sources. Prepare a report which you can share with your class. How does sharing this information help you? How does it help your classmates?

CHAPTER 4

China: Its Land and People

THE GREAT WALL

The sky looks lower when you stand on top of Badaling

And the mountain peaks look smaller

With the meandering Great Wall

Reigning over them

—Marshal Chen Yi

CHAPTER FOCUS

You will read about the climate, geography, and population of China in this chapter. As you read, think about how climate and geography affect the ways Chinese meet their needs. Think also about how the ways Chinese meet these needs are the same and different from the ways Canadians do. Try to answer these questions:

• How does China's geography affect the way people interact with each other?

• What special problems does China's climate create for its population?

• How have the Chinese solved the problem of communicating with the country's many groups of people?

THINK ABOUT IT

1. Where you live and how you live are affected by the geography of your home area. How does the geography of the area you live in affect the way you dress, the foods you eat, your home, and the things you do for fun?

Population Distribution of China

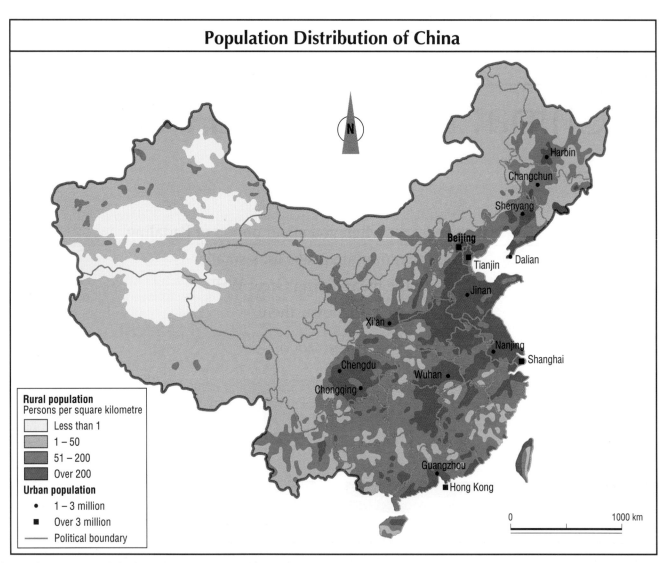

China is one of the largest countries in the world. It is also the most populated. As you can see, its people are concentrated in certain parts of the country. Why do you think people live where they do?

China, One of the World's Largest Countries

China is the third largest country in the world. It is over half the size of Russia, slightly smaller than Canada, slightly larger than the United States. Although China is physically smaller than Canada, it has many more people than Canada. Canada's population is just over 26 000 000. China's population is over 1 000 000 000—about 40 times bigger than Canada's. Almost one-quarter of the world's people live in China. The Chinese government reported that in 1992 there were more babies born in China—27 000 000—than make up the entire population of Canada!

FACTS ON CHINA

Capital City: Beijing

Population: 1 072 220 000

Area: 9 596 961 km²

Major Airports: Beijing Capital International Airport; Shanghai Honqiao International Airport

Official Language: Putonghua (Mandarin)

Religions: Confucianism, Buddhism, **Daoism**, Christianity

Physical Features of China

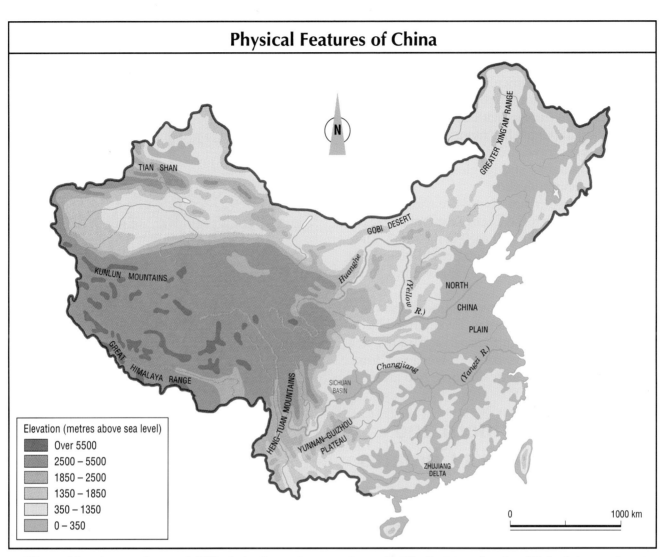

Elevation (metres above sea level)
- Over 5500
- 2500 – 5500
- 1850 – 2500
- 1350 – 1850
- 350 – 1350
- 0 – 350

0   1000 km

Natural barriers made travel difficult in the early centuries and still affect travel today. High plateaus, deserts, mountains, and jungles are some of China's physical characteristics.

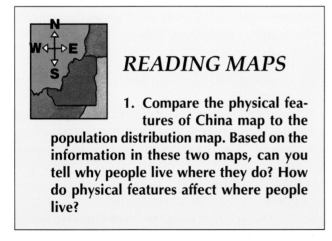

READING MAPS

1. Compare the physical features of China map to the population distribution map. Based on the information in these two maps, can you tell why people live where they do? How do physical features affect where people live?

Natural barriers have always created challenges for China's peoples. The *far west* of China is cut off from the rest of the world by high plateaus and

huge deserts. The *southwestern* and *southern* boundaries of China pass through high mountains, deep river gorges, and dense jungles. The *eastern* boundary of China is the sea, which is subject to violent storms.

To the *north* are vast plains and forests where nomads once lived. To discourage the nomads from attacking, the Chinese built walls to mark their territory. These walls were later joined together to form the Great Wall of China. It stretches for over 2000 km, from the seacoast in the east to the Gobi Desert in the west. It is so big astronauts can see it when they orbit the Earth! To see the Great Wall, look back at the picture on page 25. Look also at the map on page 13.

Geography can make it easier for people to move around. It can also isolate people. In Canada, the St. Lawrence and Mackenzie rivers are physical features that helped people of the past to travel easily. But, the Rocky Mountains and great distances across the prairies were barriers. These features often made it difficult for people to communicate. One reason for building the railway was to help Canadians interact with each other.

Like Canada, China has rivers that helped people in the past travel. Yet China's high plateaus, deserts, mountains, and jungles were barriers to travel and communication.

China's three major rivers are the Huanghe (Yellow) in the north, the Changjiang (Yangzi) in the centre, and the Zhujiang (Pearl) in the south. They flow from east to west. They provide excellent transportation routes, but they make north-south contact difficult.

The richest land in China is found along these major rivers and their **deltas**. Productive land is located in two places in the east, and in the rich red soil of the Sichuan basin in western China. Most of China's people live in these two areas.

How Are Northern and Southern China's Climates Different?

A river called the Changjiang divides China into north and south. North China is very different from South China. North of the Changjiang, there are hot, dry summers and cold, dry winters. This climate is similar to the prairie regions of Canada. Common crops in northern China are cotton, wheat, corn, barley, soybeans, and peanuts.

South of the Changjiang, there are hot, humid summers and cool, dry winters. The land is lush, and there is an abundance of water. Crops such as rice, tea, vegetables and mulberry (for silkworms) are grown.

Climate helps determine the lifestyles of the people in northern and southern China. It helps determine the kinds of houses they live in, the clothing they wear, and the food they eat.

Comparing China's and Canada's Climates

China's climate is milder than Canada's. While all of Canada has snowfall in the winter, only the far north of China is cold and has heavy snowfalls.

The climate in this picture may remind you of another Pacific Rim country—Canada! This picture of the Summer Palace in Beijing was taken during the winter.

Southern China has a milder, wetter climate than northern China. The Lijiang River passes through this farm country in southern China.

The southern half of China rarely, if ever, has ice and snow.

Canada's weather is affected by the polar ice mass in its north. In China, weather is affected by huge deserts and **monsoon** winds. In general, Canadians need to wear warmer clothing in winter than the Chinese.

Because of the differences in climate, China produces a much larger range of fruits and vegetables than does Canada. This has made Chinese food different from Canadian food, although the two countries do have a number of crops in common.

Its varied climate means that China produces a vast range of natural products. For example, when people think of tea, bamboo, silk, and rice, they usually think of China.

China's climate has also made China the home of unique animals. The giant panda, for example, lives in China's bamboo forests. This animal has become an international symbol for China. The panda is also a symbol used by the World Wildlife Fund (WWF) to represent the world's endangered animals.

What Kinds of Problems Does Nature Cause?

All of China is subject to natural disasters such as floods, **droughts**, rains, and **typhoons**. These natural disasters affect agriculture and daily living. China is also affected by earthquakes and volcanoes. In fact, all the Pacific Rim countries are affected by earthquakes and volcanoes. For this reason, the area around the Pacific Ocean is known as *the ring of fire*. You will read about earthquakes and volcanoes from time to time in the newspaper. If you live in British Columbia, you may feel an earthquake sometime.

Lu Xiaoping (11 years old) Speaks of the Flood

My family has lived beside the Changjiang for many **generations**. *One day the rains came and didn't stop for a whole week. All of a sudden the flood came. It was the middle of the night. We were lucky to survive. We lost everything, our house, our belongings, our animals. A teacher and several schoolmates drowned. Every family in the area suffered. Now we must begin to rebuild our lives. We need places to live. We need to rebuild the school. For generations, we have had to deal with floods by rebuilding.*

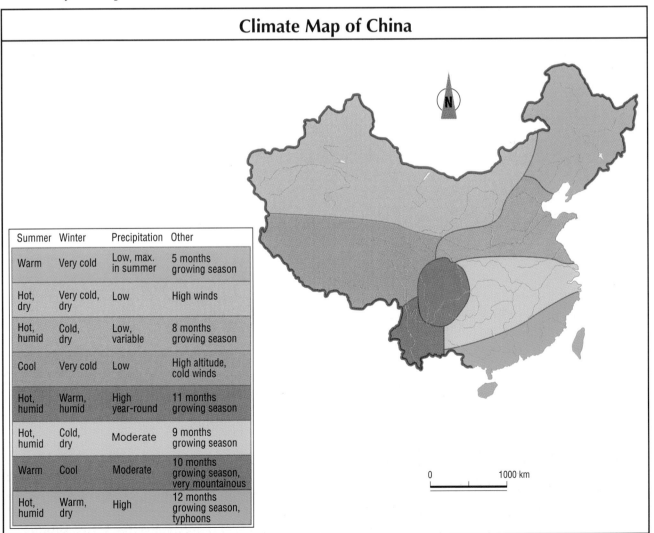

Climate Map of China

Summer	Winter	Precipitation	Other
Warm	Very cold	Low, max. in summer	5 months growing season
Hot, dry	Very cold, dry	Low	High winds
Hot, humid	Cold, dry	Low, variable	8 months growing season
Cool	Very cold	Low	High altitude, cold winds
Hot, humid	Warm, humid	High year-round	11 months growing season
Hot, humid	Cold, dry	Moderate	9 months growing season
Warm	Cool	Moderate	10 months growing season, very mountainous
Hot, humid	Warm, dry	High	12 months growing season, typhoons

0   1000 km

China is such a big country that its climate varies greatly from place to place and from season to season.

Natural Resources

Geography and climate both affect the ways Chinese meet their needs. China's natural resources also help shape the ways its people live and work. China's natural resources include oil, coal, iron, and copper. Oil and coal are natural sources of energy. They are used to power China's factories, heat many of the country's buildings and homes, and fuel the nation's ships, airplanes, trucks, and cars. Minerals like iron and copper are used to make steel, wire, and other finished products. Most of China's natural resources are used in China to

LET'S TALK ABOUT IT

1. Do you think Canada should share its resources with China? Why or why not?

help make finished products. Some of these products are used in China. Others are sold to buyers in other countries.

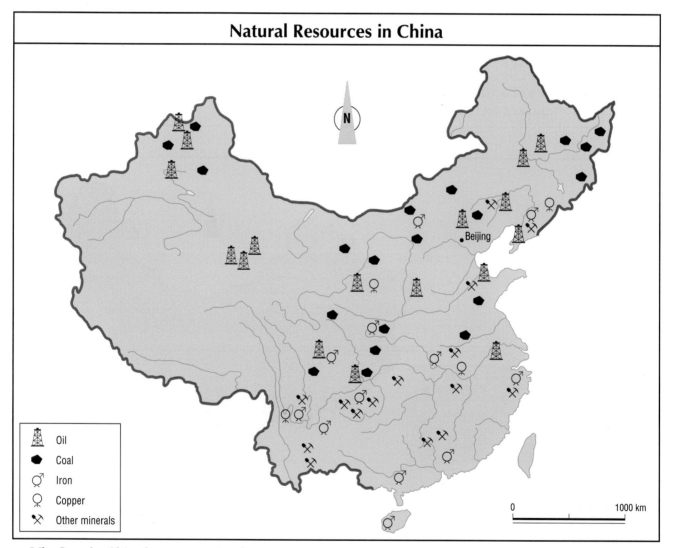

Natural Resources in China

N

Beijing

0   1000 km

Legend:
- Oil
- Coal
- Iron
- Copper
- Other minerals

Like Canada, China has many natural resources.

The Han Chinese and the National Minorities

China's population is nearly 40 times greater than that of Canada. Most people, about 92 per cent, are called Han Chinese. As you read in chapter 3, Han is the name of an early Chinese dynasty that began over 2000 years ago.

The remaining 8 per cent of China's population is made up of people from the national **minority groups**. There are 55 national minorities in China. These groups include Tibetans, Koreans, Manchus, Mongols, Dais, Lolos, Uighurs, Kazaks, Zhuangs, Huis, and Shans. These minority groups generally live in the outlying areas of China, near its borders.

The many groups of people who make up China's population have distinctive dress, languages, and customs. To solve the problem of communicating with each other, China has adopted one official language, Putonghua (Mandarin). Because China's population shares a common language, language is not a barrier between people. Having one official language does not mean that other languages are not spoken. Minority groups still speak their own languages. People can speak in the language of their choice, but business and education are conducted in Putonghua.

Although the Han outnumber other groups of people in China, mutual respect for differences between groups is a key to harmony in the country. Minority groups are free to live where they choose and to follow the lifestyle of their ancestors. Minority groups often choose to live in separate communities and keep their own languages, special clothing, and customs.

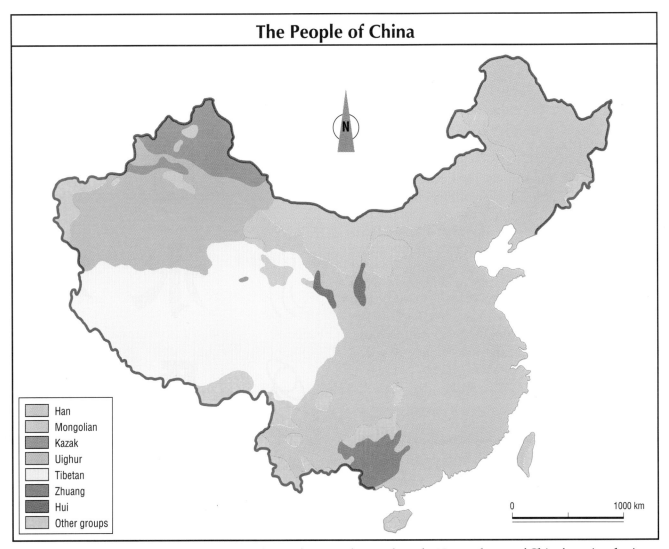

The People of China

Legend:
- Han
- Mongolian
- Kazak
- Uighur
- Tibetan
- Zhuang
- Hui
- Other groups

There are 56 different groups of people in China. This map shows where the Han and some of China's national minorities live. Compare this map with the map on page 28.

Why Do People Keep Their Own Languages?

THINK ABOUT IT

1. Canada has two official languages. Why is this important to Canadians? How does this affect people whose original language is not English or French?

Languages

Languages allow people to record their history, pass on stories to their children, and do business with each other. Language can also be used to help unite people. China's government has helped unite the country by deciding that all Chinese must be able to speak Putonghua (Mandarin).

In the world today, there are between 3000 and 4000 language groups. Of these, Chinese and English are spoken by the greatest number of people.

Like all languages, Chinese is a combination of written symbols and sounds. The Chinese language is very different from English or French, however. Chinese words, called characters, are actually pictures. They are pictures of things and ideas. Parts of the pictures give the reader some hints about the sound of the character. When learning Chinese, people must be prepared for a lot of memory work to match pictures and sounds clearly. People who have learned to read using our alphabet learn to sound out words. In Chinese, this is not possible. Students have to look in a dictionary or ask a teacher for help in pronouncing a new character.

Writing

There is one common written language for the whole of China. It started with China's earliest people, who drew a picture language on tortoise shells and the bones of cattle. Later, using brush and ink, this picture language changed and was written on thin bamboo strips. In this way, Chinese writing came to be written from top to bottom in straight lines.

Several of these bamboo strips were held together with leather thongs to form a book. Later, when paper was invented, the habit of writing from top to bottom was kept. People also learned to write from right to left. Because we write English from left to right, the Chinese, who invented paper and printing, seem to have the process backward. But, since the Chinese *invented* the process, a good question to ask is just who is doing things backward!

Unlike English, Chinese does not have an alphabet. Instead, it has over 40 000 characters! To be able to write or to read the newspaper, people must learn about 3000 to 5000 characters. They must memorize the sound of each character.

People everywhere in the world need and want to communicate with one another. Ancient Chinese symbols are an example of people's desire to record events and tell stories.

Speaking

A dialect is a form of speech from a special region in a country. For example, people from Newfoundland speak a dialect of English that is different than the English spoken in Alberta. Have you ever noticed that tv actors from England sound quite different from American actors? This is because of the way they pronounce words. Spoken Chinese is quite different from written Chinese. Spoken Chinese has five main dialects and over 100 sub-dialects.

What do you suppose the people in this photograph are talking about?

In modern China, the standard or national language is Putonghua. It used to be called Mandarin. Putonghua is spoken by more than 70 per cent of the people.

Nearly all Chinese speak both Putonghua and their own local dialect. The national language is taught in school. The native dialect is usually learned at home. People speak their native dialects so they can pass their histories and stories on to their children.

A large number of Chinese Canadians speak Guangdonghua (Cantonese), a dialect from south China. This is the region where most of their ancestors came from. You can hear Guangdonghua being spoken in towns and cities throughout Canada.

THINK ABOUT IT

1. **How might learning more than one language help people?**

In China, the written language is the same all across the country. The way people say the words may be different in various parts of China.

A LOOK BACK

China's history and geography have affected its people. China's natural barriers made it difficult for the early Chinese to communicate with people outside of their country. This isolation allowed the Chinese to develop a special way of life. But it did not allow the Chinese to exchange ideas and goods with the rest of the world. Isolation prevented China from sharing in the new knowledge of other countries.

Within China, there were also physical barriers between people. It was especially difficult for people in northern and southern China, for example, to communicate or travel to the other parts of China.

Geography also affects where people live and how they earn their living. Most of China's population lives along the major river deltas in eastern coastal China, or in the Sichuan basin in western China. Because of the rich soil in these areas, many of the Chinese people are involved in agriculture.

China's varied climate allows the Chinese to grow a variety of crops, such as tea, bamboo, and rice. The moderate climate in some areas of China also allows the production of silk because the silkworm can survive there.

For centuries, the Chinese people have rebuilt homes and towns after the monsoon rains which bring heavy floods, or after earthquakes.

China is home to over 1 000 000 000 people. Most Chinese are descendants of the Han Dynasty and call themselves the Han. Fifty-five national minorities also live in China. The attitude of respect for others' differences allows these people to live in harmony. These groups all share a common language, Putonghua (Mandarin), which helps people to communicate easily.

A LOOK AHEAD

- People express their beliefs and values in many ways. In the next chapter, you will look at some Chinese customs and traditions.
- Customs and traditions influence the Chinese to think, act, and behave toward themselves and others in special ways.
- There are many festivals and holidays in China.
- Customs and traditions are a result of people's history and geography. The next chapter discusses specific customs and traditions which have developed in China over time.

Questions

1. The Chinese have always relied on their rivers for transportation. In Canada, do we use our main rivers for the same purpose? If so, how? If not, why not? You may want to do some research to help you answer this question.

2. In China, the weather brings on many natural disasters. What are some of these and how do they affect people's lives? In Canada, are we affected by natural disasters? What are they, and how do they affect us?

3. In what parts of China do most people live? Explain, in several sentences, why this is so. Compare your information on China to a population map of Canada. What are the differences and similarities you can find?

Activities

1. Do you speak more than one language? What is it like to know another language? How does that make you feel? Can you teach the members of your class a few words of greeting in your second or third language? Share your experience of learning a second language with a small group.

2. Invite a person who can speak and write Chinese to your class. Ask him or her to teach you to speak and to write some Chinese. Ask what it is like to learn English as a second language.

CHAPTER 5

Special Customs and Traditions

One generation builds the road

That the next one travels on

—Old Chinese Saying

CHAPTER FOCUS

Many customs and traditions are practised in China. Many of these are based on the traditional need for harmony. Other customs are the result of historical beliefs and influences. The festivals and holidays you will read about are Chinese ways of celebrating traditions. Think about how studying this information can help you learn what is important to Chinese people. Try to answer these questions:

- What beliefs are important to Chinese people?

- What are some ways the Chinese people celebrate their respect for others?

- How do the customs, beliefs, festivals, and holidays of the Chinese help them meet their needs for social harmony and communication with others?

THINK ABOUT IT

1. As you learned when reading about Eileen and her family, customs and traditions influence the way people meet their needs. Think about your family, your school, and your community's traditions. What are some customs and traditions which your friends and family practise?

2. Why are customs and traditions important?

Many Chinese work to keep harmony in their world. Buildings and other human creations are made to fit in with the environment.

How Do the Chinese Meet Their Need for Harmony?

All people have needs. We need food, water, and shelter to stay alive. Many Chinese believe that we also need to be in harmony with our world, and with each other. One way to be in harmony is through customs and traditions.

In every country, customs and traditions are important to people. If we think about Canada, we can see that there are many different customs and traditions at work in our country. For example, some people believe Sunday is a holy day, and do not work on that day. Others believe Saturday is a holy day. Some groups also have organizations to teach young people about their groups' customs and traditions.

In China, many people believe that harmony can be achieved by behaving in certain ways. For example, people stay in harmony with their bodies by practising tai-chi, a kind of **martial art**. Tai-chi is a way of exercising both your body and your mind. With a healthy body, you are less likely to get ill or be unhappy. Also, many of the festivals in

China encourage harmony by bringing people together to learn more about each other and to take part in events together.

Tai-chi exercises the body and the mind. Many Chinese believe that tai-chi keeps them in harmony with their body.

RESEARCH

1. **Chinese martial arts, like tai-chi, are exercises that help to keep your body and mind healthy. They are becoming quite popular in Canada. Can you think of why?**

2. **Look up martial arts in your phone book. Phone one or two of the clubs listed. Find out where the martial art came from. In your notebook, make a chart that lists martial arts and countries that they came from.**

Kite Flying for Harmony

Have you ever spent a windy spring or summer day in the park flying a kite? Did you know that the Chinese were flying kites as early as 500 BC? The Chinese had kites 2000 years before Europeans did.

Chinese tradition says that the legendary god of artisans, Gongshu Pan, flew some of the first kites. He made kites shaped like birds, and his kites could do somersaults. Perhaps the first person to build a kite was a philosopher named Mo Di, who spent three years building a special kite. His followers, called *Mohists*, sometimes constructed kites for military uses.

In the 600s and 700s, the Chinese created musical kites. A "wind zither," or a "wind psalter," is a kite with a bamboo strip attached. When the wind blows through the bamboo strip, the kite makes a whistling or a harp sound.

Kites were used by a religious group in China. Daoists would fly a kite and think of the harmony between the kite and the wind. Daoists lived in the mountains, where the winds were suitable for kite flying. While flying their kites, Daoists would think about how the kite was touching the wind, and how they must loosen or tighten the string as the wind changed. Daoists also imagined that their thoughts were flying with their kites.

Early Daoists imagined that their thoughts were flying with their kites. Now, people around the world enjoy making and flying kites.

The Daoists also experimented with kites that could lift people off the ground. These human-lifting kites were the first hang-gliders. These large kites were used throughout China by the 1200s.

Today, Chinese still love to fly kites. They fly traditional bird-shaped kites, as well as kites shaped like centipedes, frogs, butterflies, dragons, and many other real and imaginary creatures. Some dragon kites can roll their eyes and move their paws and tails!

RESEARCH

1. **In groups of two or three, research how to make a kite. Make the kite and fly it! Record your thoughts as you flew the kite.**

2. **Find some pictures of early Chinese kites. Copy one of your favourite patterns into your notebook.**

The Buddha was the founder of Buddhism. The Buddha taught that all life is sacred.

Buddhist Beliefs in China

Chinese beliefs have been influenced by religious ideas from other countries. These ideas also have helped the Chinese to meet their need for harmony. Beliefs related to Buddhism, Islam, and Christianity have influenced China.

Buddhism is a religion that came from India to China 2000 years ago. This religion was started by Siddhartha Gautama, who came from a very rich Indian family. He left his riches to find a different life. He became known as the Buddha.

All life is sacred to a Buddhist. Buddhists believe that a person is forbidden to kill anything, even a small animal. Another belief is that people live through many lifetimes. Buddhists believe that after you die, you will be born again and again. Each time, you will try to become a better person, until you reach *nirvana*, or perfection. This belief is called reincarnation. Buddhism changed the way many Chinese thought about life and death.

Buddhism became an important religion in China. Today, various forms of Buddhism are practised in several Pacific Rim countries, including Canada.

How Islam Came to China

Another religion, called **Islam**, came to China from the Middle East.

One day in the early summer of 651 AD, the people of Guangzhou (Canton) saw a strange sight on the Zhujiang. It was an Arab ship that had come all the way from the Persian Gulf. On board were an ambassador from Baghdad and a group of merchants. They had come to China to open trade relations. They were merchants and **Muslims**, followers of a new faith called Islam.

Although the ambassador had come to China by sea, it was not the only route to China. Other traders from the Middle East reached Changan by traveling through the high mountain passes of Central Asia. They, too, brought with them the teachings of Islam.

In 751 AD, when the emperor of China was faced with a major rebellion, he asked for help from his neighbours in Central Asia. Many of the soldiers who came from Central Asia in answer to his call were Muslims. A number of them stayed in China. They spread the Islamic faith in northwest China, in the provinces of Gansu and Ningxia.

Nearly 600 years later, when the Mongol armies under Kublai Khan conquered China, the Khan's Muslim troops advanced into southwest China, to Yunnan province. Many of these troops stayed and married into local families. Thus, the Islamic faith was spread into southwest China.

Today, the major centres of Muslim population are in Yunnan, Gansu, and Ningxia provinces. Muslims in China are considered to be a national minority and are called the Hui. There are an estimated 20 million Muslims in China today.

How Did Christianity Come to China?

Missionaries from France and Italy first brought Christianity to China in the 1200s. Christianity is 2000 years old. Its holy book is the *Bible*, and Christians follow the teachings of Jesus Christ.

Missionaries from Europe, America, and Canada had strong influences on the development of the Chinese education system from 1905 to 1949. They built many schools, hospitals, and nursing stations.

In 1949, a new Chinese government decided it would be better for China if the foreigners left. Missionaries were not welcome anymore. Many returned home. Some were imprisoned.

In the 1970s, the Chinese government decided to make China more open again. They welcomed back some of these earlier Christian missionaries, to visit places where they once lived, and to see old friends.

Muslims in China worship in mosques like this one. There are about 20 million Muslims in China today.

Traditions in Festivals

Religion plays a role in some Chinese festivals. However, some festivals are based on other beliefs and events.

During the year, there are many festivals and holidays in China. Some of these festivals started with religious traditions, like Christmas in Canada. Many festivals are to give thanks for the well-being of the people, like Canadian Thanksgiving. Other festivals are to remember loved ones or national heroes who have died, like Remembrance Day in Canada. All festivals include **rituals** and feasting.

Spring Festival (Chinese New Year)

Spring Festival is the most important festival of the year. It starts off the Chinese New Year. Spring Festival comes between mid-January and late February. It is a family holiday, similar to Christmas in Canada.

The old year is chased away by setting off firecrackers. The new year is usually welcomed in by dragon or lion dances in the community. People

Spring Festival is a time to begin the new year with happy celebrations.

clean their houses, pay their debts, wear new clothes, prepare feasts, exchange gifts, and visit each other. Children receive **lucky money** and have a long holiday from school. This is a time for family get-togethers. Many Chinese Canadians celebrate this festival in Canada.

Festivals are fun. People celebrate some special events by sharing in games, special foods, and activities. Most Chinese festivals, like this one in Guangzhou, include parades.

Lantern Festival began as a time to pay respect to the gods.

Lantern Festival

Lantern Festival follows very soon after Spring Festival. Traditionally, lanterns were lit to pay respect to the gods. This festival is celebrated by large public displays of beautiful lanterns and big fireworks. Lantern Festival is not an official holiday anymore, so people celebrate during the evening, when they are not working.

At Qingming, people pay respect to their ancestors.

Qingming

Qingming marks the beginning of spring. It is a time for planting farm crops and gardens. It is also a time to visit and tend the graves of ancestors. People pay their respects to their ancestors and prepare a feast in their honour. People show their respect by bowing toward the grave. Then the family enjoys a large meal. Qingming is not a holiday in China, even though it is a celebration. It is a day to remember loved ones who have passed away.

May 1 is the holiday to honour workers in China.

May Day

The first day of May is a holiday. This holiday honours the contributions that workers make to society. May Day is celebrated in many other countries of the world. It is called International Workers' Day. In Canada, we have a different holiday for workers: Labour Day is the first Monday of September, every year.

Dragon Boat Festival welcomes summer and reminds people of the story of Qu Yuan.

Dragon Boat Festival

Dragon Boat Festival is on the fifth day of the fifth month in the lunar calendar (June). This day welcomes summer. It features races between long, thin boats, decorated to look like dragons.

There is a story behind the Dragon Boat Festival. Once there was a loyal government official named Qu Yuan. He fell into a river. When the village people heard what had happened, they put boats in the water to try to save him, but he drowned. Then the people made dumplings and threw them in the river. They hoped the river dragon and the fish would eat the dumplings instead of their friend's body.

Ever since then, the Chinese have remembered Qu Yuan. They keep his memory alive. As well as having dragon boat races, families eat *zongzi*, special dumplings wrapped in bamboo leaves.

Children's Day

Children's Day is celebrated on June 1. It is a special day to honour children, who are China's future. It is a school holiday. Because the weather is warm, there are many special outdoor activities in the parks, zoos, and Children's Palaces. The palaces are places where children can study arts and crafts, music, and martial arts after school.

Children's Day is a holiday to celebrate each new generation.

National Day is the birthday of the People's Republic of China.

Zhongyong Festival is very old. People go to the mountains to honour their ancestors and ask for the protection of their children.

National Day

National Day on October 1 is a public holiday in China. It is China's birthday. This was the day when Chairman Mao Zedong proclaimed the founding of the People's Republic of China in 1949. There are celebrations and parades all over the country.

Moon or Mid-Autumn Festival

Moon or Mid-autumn Festival falls on the fifteenth day of the eighth month. It is a time to thank the gods for the harvest and to admire the beautiful full moon. Hundreds of years ago, some Chinese **peasants** used this occasion to rise up against a **tyrannical** warlord during harvest time. To unite the people for the uprising, the peasants passed around messages hidden in little round cakes. The rich warlord was enjoying the beauty of the harvest moon, and was unprepared for trouble. The people were successful in driving out the tyrant. To this day, the Chinese remember this event with sweet round cakes, called mooncakes. There is also a special feast to celebrate the harvest.

Zhongyong Festival

Zhongyong Festival is in the fall. According to ancient tradition, parents were to take all their children and go into the mountains to keep them from harm. They would spend a day there. Now, on this festival day, people visit the graves of their ancestors. They pray, asking their ancestors to protect them from evil and look after them. Zhongyong Festival is not an official holiday.

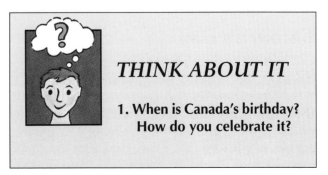

THINK ABOUT IT

1. When is Canada's birthday? How do you celebrate it?

A LOOK BACK

The Chinese people have many customs and traditions which are important to them. Some of these customs and traditions involve exercising body and mind. Others are festivals which may involve prayers, feasting, or other rituals. Some of the customs and traditions in China help the Chinese people be in harmony with the world and each other. Other customs and traditions allow people to celebrate after hard work, pay respect to gods, honour ancestors, or celebrate their nation's birthday.

Customs and traditions are often celebrated within special events called festivals. Festivals provide occasions for families and friends to get together and celebrate. Festivals also provide opportunities for the elder people in China to pass customs and traditions to the younger people in their country.

Customs and traditions are based on ideas from many sources. Some ideas are religious in nature, others are based on historical events. Several Chinese customs and traditions are similar to ones practised by Canadians.

By studying Chinese customs and traditions, we can learn more about the ways in which Chinese people meet some of their needs. We can also learn about the ways in which Canadians and Chinese meet their needs in similar ways.

A LOOK AHEAD

- Customs and traditions are ways of life that have been followed for many, many years. Sometimes, events in our countries change the way we live. Customs are sometimes forgotten because they no longer seem important.
- As China has developed stronger relationships with other Pacific Rim neighbours, customs practised in China have changed.
- As customs in China change, people in China change other aspects of the way they live.

Questions

1. Answer the Chapter Focus questions on page 37. Compare your answers with a partner. Are there differences in your answers? What are these differences? Why do these differences occur?

2. Which Chinese belief or religion is most interesting to you? Why?

3. Canadians and Chinese have festivals and holidays. Which are the ones that are most similar? How are they similar and how are they different?

4. If you moved to China, what would you do on July 1?

Activities

1. Find out more about one religion practised in China and one in Canada. Record any special rules that are followed by the people who practise these religions. Share your findings with a group.

2. Make a chart which identifies six festivals in China and six in Canada. Beside each festival, identify the needs that are being met when people participate in these festivals.

CHAPTER 6

A Changing Way of Life

It is easier to rule a country

Than to run a family

—*Old Chinese Saying*

CHAPTER FOCUS

China's society is changing. Some of the changes are the result of communication with other countries and sharing new technology with them. As you will learn, some changes are occurring rapidly, while other changes are very gradual. Because of China's long history and its many traditions and customs, some Chinese people are dissatisfied with the speed at which change is occurring. As you read, think about how these changes might affect the Chinese people, especially in terms of creating conflict between traditional and modern ways. Try to answer these questions:

- How does change affect people?
- What are families like in China?
- What kinds of houses do the Chinese live in?
- How do the Chinese earn a living?
- What do the Chinese do for fun?
- Do the Chinese have different needs than Canadians? Why do they have some needs that are the same?

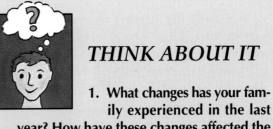

THINK ABOUT IT

1. What changes has your family experienced in the last year? How have these changes affected the way your family lives?

2. Record your feelings about the changes your family experienced.

MINI STUDY: *The Changing Family in China*

In this Mini Study, you will read about two different kinds of families in China. One is a traditional family, and one is a modern family. Think about why the family is changing in China, and how the change is affecting the way Chinese meet their needs.

Traditionally, Chinese families were very large. Today, China's government wants families to have only one child.

In old China, teenagers often married at age 14 or 15. Usually, the parents arranged the marriages, sometimes with the help of **matchmakers**. In old China, men were allowed to take more than one wife.

In the old days, a man often had two or more wives.

Since 1949, marriage in China has changed. One man may have only one wife. Young people can marry for love, instead of being matched up. Men and women must be in their 20s before they can marry. Young people, however, still look for approval from their parents.

In traditional Chinese families, the oldest man was the head of the family. Newlyweds lived with the husband's family. A typical family at that time consisted of three or more generations. In modern China, usually only two generations live together.

In the old days in China, families tended to be large. Families often had six or more children. Even though many babies died because families were too poor to properly feed and care for them, families tried to have more babies. Parents believed that if they had a large family, then some of their children would survive to care for them in their old age.

As living conditions changed for the better, more children survived to become adults. But people continued to have large families. China's population began to grow very large. This meant that there were more people for the country to feed.

In 1979, the government announced the **One Child policy**. Couples who had only one child were given better jobs, housing, and other privileges. Couples with more than one child did not receive these benefits.

All this has changed family life in China. Some older people may not like the changes that have occurred. Some younger people may not like to be told how many children they can have.

There has been another change in Chinese family life. Today, both parents usually work outside the home. In the past, mothers and grandmothers looked after the children at home. Today, many families use day-care centres. **Child care** is now something Chinese parents think of in a different way than their parents did.

Questions

1. If you were a grandparent in China, what would you think of the One Child policy? Explain your answer.

2. Describe how you think your parents would react if the government told them how many children they could have. What would their reaction be based on? What if food was very limited? What might this situation tell you about individual and group concerns?

3. Do you think families should be large or should they have only one child? Why?

THINK ABOUT IT

1. In old China, parents and matchmakers arranged marriages. Now, most people marry for love. In your own tradition, how do people decide to marry? How has this changed over time?

2. List advantages and disadvantages of arranged marriages.

In the past, women were not allowed many work choices. Today, they may choose from many kinds of work. What kind of work does this woman do?

The Changing Role of Women in China

One hundred years ago, Chinese women were regarded as **inferior** to men. Their jobs were to care for their husbands, have children, and look after their families.

Confucianism taught that women were second-class people. A woman was expected to obey her father, her husband, and her adult son. In her own house, she was expected also to obey her mother-in-law. One of a wife's most important jobs was to produce a son. If she did not do that, her husband could divorce her or find a second wife.

In Confucian society, boy children were highly valued, but girl children were not. Sometimes girls were killed at birth.

In 1950, the marriage law was changed so that Chinese women were given equal rights. This changed traditional beliefs and gave women more freedom under the law. Many women took positions of leadership in the new China. Women can now work as doctors, engineers, scientists, teachers, or other professionals. They no longer have to depend on their husbands for support. They can now support themselves. This gives them a new way of looking at their lives. They are becoming more equal to their husbands.

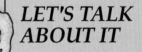

LET'S TALK ABOUT IT

1. When today's grandmothers were young, they had fewer choices than girls in Canada do today.

(a) What are two things girls can do now that a grandmother probably could not do when she was young?

(b) Why is it important for women to have more choices now?

(c) How does having choices help women?

(d) How does having choices help men?

This woman had her feet broken and bound when she was a little girl because tiny feet were considered beautiful. As a result, she could not run, skip, or play.

Why Were Women's Feet Bound?

In earlier times in China, wealthy city girls had their feet bound. The four small toes were bent back under the foot and held there with strong strips of cloth. The feet were broken and stunted. Women could not walk properly. Men thought the most beautiful women had feet that could fit into a teacup. Poets described them walking as "willows in the wind." Women with unbound feet were considered ugly, and hard to "marry off."

Peasants did not bind the feet of girls and women because they had to move swiftly in the fields as they worked on the farms.

Western people who went to China were shocked at the practice of footbinding. They helped organize societies to have it stopped.

MINI STUDY: *Mrs. Lam Remembers*

In the following Mini Study, you will read the words of a Chinese woman remembering her life. Mrs. Lam was born in 1906. Now she lives in a retirement home in Hong Kong. As you read, think about how her life has changed over time.

I was never taught to read or write. I am just speaking my story, and a young woman is writing it down for you. It is a true story.

My father was a seaman who drowned. After his death, we became very poor. There was only my mother to look after us. There were eight of us, all girls.

Mama sent my three youngest sisters to live with my grandmother. Two of them starved to death, I heard. The third one survived. She lives in Canada and has grown-up children now.

My mother was heartbroken that she didn't have a son, a male **heir**. Mama sold three of us so that she would have enough money to buy a son. The son could then carry on the family name. The boy was 12 years old when my mother bought him.

My older sister was sold as a **concubine**, or secondary wife, when she was 14. My twin sister and

I were 10. My twin was sold to one family and I was sold to another. I never saw her again.

I was talented. I could sing and dance, and the family that bought me hired teachers for singing and dancing. It would have been nice to learn to read and write, too, but I guess that wouldn't make any money.

When I was 12, I began performing on stage. I made lots of money, but I was never allowed to keep any for myself, or to send any to my family.

For four years, I sang and danced and made money for the people who bought me. Then, when I was 16 years old, I agreed to become the concubine of a very rich man who paid for me to be released. I belonged to him, then. I spent five years with him and was happy. We did not have any children, though. He died, and then I had no one to look after me.

Soon afterward, I became the concubine of an army general, but he was later killed in war. I married five times after that, but each time, my husband died or was killed. I never had any children. I was told that it was punishment for the life I led.

continued

Mini Study continued

When Mrs. Lam was a child, boys were valued above girls in China. But today, Chinese girls have better opportunities than in the past.

I do not have children to care for me now. Sometimes I feel sad and lonely.

I have seen many changes in China since I was born. Life is so different for women now! They do not have to sell their children. Girl children can have an education. They can choose their own husbands! They can choose whether to have children! They are more independent, and do not have to depend on their husbands. One niece told me that she and her husband have an equal relationship! I don't know what that means. I always had to serve my husbands.

Times have really changed from when I was her age. Sometimes I wish I was born 50 years later! I cannot imagine what it is like to grow up as a girl these days.

Questions

1. Talk to your grandmother or a senior woman you know in your neighbourhood. Ask her what it was like to grow up as a girl when she was your age. Think about the similarities between her life and yours.

2. Talk to your grandfather or a senior man, and ask the same questions.

3. Mrs. Lam has seen many changes in her life. What changes in the role of women does Mrs. Lam seem to think are the most positive? Why do you think this is so important to Mrs. Lam?

In China, people live in a variety of dwellings. In cities, modern apartments are popular because they are comfortable.

Changing Homes

For generations, rich Chinese families lived in huge houses. They had several **courtyards**, with walls surrounding them for privacy. Poor families lived in small rooms with shared courtyard, cooking, and washing facilities. In the cities, houses were built of bricks with tiled roofs. In the villages, houses were built of mud and earth with thatched roofs.

Today, there are still many people who live in old-style housing with shared conveniences. In the cities, more modern apartment buildings are being built, with kitchens, bathrooms, running water, and electricity.

In rural areas, some people still live in mud houses with thatched roofs, but many now have brick houses with tiled roofs. Although not everyone has running water, electricity is available.

LET'S TALK ABOUT IT

1. People live in a variety of housing. In a group, list the types of housing you know about in China and in Canada. Which type of housing do you prefer?

In old-style housing, kitchens are not very modern.

Houseboats on the Lijiang provide floating homes. People who live on houseboats may earn money by fishing, harvesting water plants, and shipping goods from place to place.

Living on a Houseboat

Although homes in China are changing, many Chinese people still live in traditional homes, including houseboats and caves. In southern and eastern China, many people live on houseboats. They may live on a boat their whole lives. Many make their living from fishing, shipping, or harvesting plants that grow in the sea or in the rivers.

The boats may be small *sampans*, or *junks*. They are powered by oil-powered engines and sails. Light comes from an oil lamp. People cook using charcoal **braziers**.

At night, the boats are tied up. People go ashore to visit, shop, go to school, or go for entertainment.

Living in a Cave

Other unique houses in China are caves! In northwest China, the land is just right for digging into the hillsides to construct beautiful cave homes. The yellow earth, called loess, is easy to dig into yet does not crumble or cave in.

By tunneling into cliffs or hillsides, people can create a very comfortable home. The cave opening is fitted with a wall containing windows, door, and chimney. The cave can be wired for electricity and have indoor plumbing. Cool in summer, warm in winter, these homes are so unusual that tourists visit Yan'an to see them. Caves provide very good housing for thousands of people.

As the population increases, creating decent housing for everyone will be an important problem for the Chinese to solve.

Some Chinese have very comfortable homes in caves.

How Are Household Needs in China Changing?

No matter where people live in China, they have basic needs and wants. Chinese people are asking for items which make their lives more comfortable. Because of the cost of these items in China, however, many of the products are considered **luxury items**.

Read the following interview with Yu Chao to learn about household items in China. Chao is one of the illustrators of this book. She moved to Canada from China two years ago.

The large billboard in this photo advertises the kinds of products the Chinese would like to have in their homes.

Q: *What would you say are the top three household items wanted by Chinese citizens?*

A: "People want microwave ovens, videocassette recorders (VCRs) and clothes dryers, but only some people in China have these items because they are expensive. Although some older people may be able to afford these items, they would rather save their money. Some younger people do not want to wait the long time it takes to save for these things, so they borrow money to buy them. Older people do not think this is a good idea."

Q: *Would you say these items are luxuries in Canada, too?*

A: "No. In my apartment in Canada, I have a microwave oven and a VCR. My apartment building has a clothes dryer for me to use. I think many people in Canada have these items. When I tell my family in China about these things, they are surprised. Some think I am rich!"

THINK ABOUT IT

1. In China, younger people tend to be impatient to own the more expensive household items, while older Chinese people tend to save their money and do without the modern items. Does this happen in Canada? How do you know?

Some items in Yu Chao's apartment in Canada would be considered luxuries in China.

This young woman works in a carpet factory in China. Because China and Canada are trading partners, it is possible that this carpet might end up in a home in Halifax, Toronto, or Calgary!

How Do Chinese Earn Their Livings?

The ways in which people make their livings are affected by a country's history and geography. Because of its limited agricultural land and large population, most of China's people are involved in agriculture.

In the past, farming needed many strong hands and long, long hours. Many people did not go to school. Instead, they learned only the skills needed to maintain their family's traditional way of life. Besides that, Confucian beliefs taught that people should have their "place" and not try to change.

Today, 80 per cent of China's population still live in rural areas and make their living in agriculture. This is partly due to the need for food, and partly due to the slow rate of change in farming methods. China did not use many of the modern machines and methods introduced in countries such as Canada until recently.

China's long period of isolation from the rest of the world also meant that it did not trade many products with other nations. As a result, while other countries in the world were building huge factories to meet their citizens' demands for modern goods, China stayed with traditional trade

How Chinese Earn Their Livings

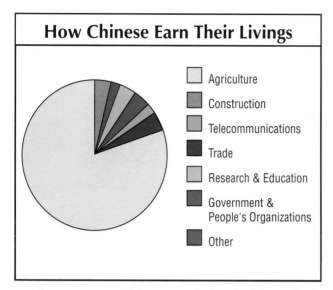

- Agriculture
- Construction
- Telecommunications
- Trade
- Research & Education
- Government & People's Organizations
- Other

There are more Chinese people involved in agriculture than in any other occupation, because China has chosen traditional farming methods. As a result, Chinese farming requires many workers.

items, such as tea, ginseng, rice, and silk. As you have just read in the interview with Yu Chao, younger Chinese people are now asking for more modern goods, such as VCRs, microwaves, and clothes dryers. Because of the demands of its citizens, and because of stronger trade relationships with other countries, China is now building more factories.

In the future, more of China's population will be involved in jobs outside of agriculture. Recently, people have been allowed to have small businesses of their own. Also, more and more jobs require Chinese workers to learn new technical skills.

All jobs in China, however, are protected by the Chinese government. The laws make sure that from the time a Chinese person starts to work, he or she will always have a job, enough to eat, and will enjoy benefits such as medicare. Chinese citizens are protected from poverty by these laws. Could these kinds of laws work in Canada? Why or why not?

Some agricultural products are sold at open-air markets like this one. Here, spices, dried eels, and other foods are bought and sold.

The Chinese don't work all the time! Once a week they relax and do something fun, like skating.

What Do the Chinese Do for Fun?

All workers and students in China have one day each week to relax and have fun. Today, recreational activities are much the same as in Canada. The Chinese enjoy movies, theatre, sports, music, dancing, painting, chess, outings, visits to places of interest, storytelling and, of course, television! Some of these activities can be enjoyed by the young as well as the old.

Children's Palaces are special places for young people to spend time. These provide games and sports facilities.

Another activity which is not only enjoyable but meets a basic need is eating in a restaurant. The Chinese love of food has been developed into a form of art. For some Chinese, the beautiful display of food is almost as important as eating the food.

These children are spending their one day away from school swimming in the Lijiang.

The Chinese circus is very popular. It's fun to watch the performers!

A LOOK BACK

As China moves into the twenty-first century, it keeps some old traditions and changes others. During the past 100 years, there have been many changes in Chinese society. The traditional family size has been reduced, and traditional marriage matchmaking is now uncommon. Most modern Chinese families have only one child, and young people choose their own marriage partners. One thing that has not changed is the importance of the family in Chinese society.

A major change in Chinese society is the increasing chance for women to have rights equal to the rights of Chinese men. Most women now work outside the home and can choose from several kinds of jobs. This is a big change from the times of Confucianism, which taught that women were second-class persons, whose chief role was to serve the males in their families!

In China, people live in a variety of homes. For example, people may live in modern apartment buildings, mud huts, caves, and houseboats. As China's population grows, the problem of creating decent housing for all its citizens is being addressed by the Chinese government.

Traditionally, most of China's population lived and worked in agricultural communities. In modern China, this is still the case, but industries are also growing as China builds stronger economic ties with other countries. Despite increases in industry, China's people will always have to deal with the challenge of feeding its large population.

A LOOK AHEAD

• Changing technologies and new ideas affect the ways modern Chinese families meet their needs.

• The Chen family, who are described in the next chapter, has to find ways to balance tradition and new technologies or ideas, to avoid conflict in their family.

Questions

1. What do Canadians do for fun? What do you do with your family for fun? If you lived in China, what might you do differently to have a good time?

2. In the past, only mothers and grandmothers in China cared for young children. How has that changed? Is it different in Canada or the same?

3. China's society is changing, and so is Canada's. Think of one change in Canadian society. Write it down and tell whether you think the change is good or bad for Canadians, and why.

4. Write several sentences which describe what you have learned about change so far in this textbook. Remember Eileen Chu's experiences, what happened to China's government, and changes to customs and traditions when preparing your answer.

5. Sometimes laws can create conflicts between people, or even between people and their government. Can you think of an example of this from your own country, and from China?

Activities

1. Using an atlas, find a chart which identifies the kinds of work that Canadians do. Compare it to the pie graph on page 56 of your text and answer the following questions.

    (a) How do most Canadians earn their livings?

    (b) What are the similarities and differences between how Canadians and Chinese earn their livings?

    (c) List reasons why you think these similarities and differences are present.

    (d) What does this information tell you about the needs of Canadians and Chinese?

CHAPTER 7

The Chen Family in China

If family members live in harmony

Then they will prosper

—Old Chinese Saying

CHAPTER FOCUS

In this chapter, you will read about one family in China. As you read, think about how this family meets its needs, and whether this family does things in the same way that traditional Chinese families did. Try to answer these questions:

- What beliefs and traditions does the Chen family practise?

- How does the Chen family deal with changes such as changing roles for women and changes in technology?

- What conflicts between traditional and modern ways are there in the Chen family?

RESEARCH

1. Think about some of the traditions in your family.
(a) Are some of the traditions practised in your family different from the ones practised by your ancestors?
(b) How does your family deal with changes?
(c) Is there any difference between the ways younger and older people in your family think about the changes and the need for change?
(d) How does your family deal with conflicts arising from change?

The Chen Apartment

The Chens are an ordinary family living in China. They are very proud of their two-room apartment. From their front door, they can walk to another door that leads into a courtyard. An old water well stands in the centre of the courtyard. They have planted roses and a peach tree outside the door. In a small garden patch, Grandmother Chen also plants vegetables like bok choy, green onions, and parsley. Grandmother keeps a few chickens for eggs, and for meat on special occasions.

In the apartment, Mr. and Mrs. Chen share a small bedroom. They keep the whole family's belongings in this room. An old **armoire** holds clothing and bedding. Inside the armoire is a locked compartment. Valuable belongings such as jewelry are stored here. Grandmother Chen is the one who keeps the key to this lock. There is a small bedside table on Mr. Chen's side of the bed. He stacks many of his technical books there.

In the other room, there is a huge day bed, made into a sofa. At night, Grandmother Chen and Leijen, the granddaughter, share this bed. Out-of-season clothing, family photo albums, and letters from relatives are stored in a chest of drawers. On top of this chest stands the family's prized possession, a 35 cm colour television. It was a gift from visiting Canadian relatives. By themselves, the Chens could not afford a colour tv.

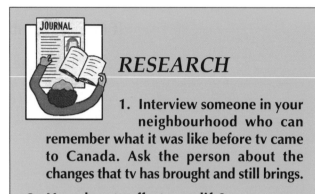

RESEARCH

1. Interview someone in your neighbourhood who can remember what it was like before tv came to Canada. Ask the person about the changes that tv has brought and still brings.

2. How does tv affect your life?

The Chens have a courtyard and garden. Grandmother Chen enjoys working in the garden.

Beside the chest of drawers stands a sewing machine. The chest is also used as a table when the sewing machine is put away. On this table is a portable radio-cassette player, also a gift from Canadian relatives. In the corner of the room is a small refrigerator, sitting on top of a cupboard for dishes. In the middle of the room is a family folding dining table, plus four chairs. There are two antique armchairs, saved from the civil war. On the walls are family portraits, pictures of overseas relatives, and a portrait of Grandfather Chen.

The most **revered** possession is the ancestral family **tablet**, on a small table, with fresh fruit offerings. This is where Grandmother Chen offers Buddhist prayers every morning and night to deceased family members. She asks them to protect her present family and to keep them well.

Grandmother Chen, Yi Weijing

Grandmother Chen had an arranged marriage when she was 17 years old. Her first son died of disease. She later had one son and four daughters. One daughter died of hunger during the Japanese invasion. One daughter lives in Hong Kong. The other two daughters are married and live in Canada. Because Grandmother Chen married a traditional Chinese doctor, she did not have to work outside of the home. She spent most of her life looking after her children, and then her granddaughter.

Grandmother Chen Speaks

I was not happy that my daughter-in-law, Shaolin, could not give me a grandson to carry on the family name. However, her husband, my son, Zhongxing, is obedient. He is a good son and keeps me happy. And I love my granddaughter, Leijen. I help to take care of the whole family. While Leijen is in school, I keep myself busy with neighbourhood affairs. I give advice to women in the neighbourhood.

This morning Grandmother Chen gets up early to pray. Today is the Mid-autumn Festival. The festival is not usually a holiday, but it is still celebrated in China. During all Chinese festivals,

Grandmother Chen is active in her neighbourhood. She gives advice to women in her neighbourhood, and attends meetings of the senior women's committee.

Grandmother Chen likes to remember the family ancestors by paying them respect in the form of a feast. She must not forget to pick up mooncakes for the family today.

When she finishes her prayers, she prepares a breakfast of rice porridge for the family. After everyone goes to work and school, she cleans the house. She tends to her plants in the yard. She notices two new buds on the peach tree. She also picks some vegetables for lunch. After lunch, she goes to the weekly meeting of the neighbourhood senior women's committee. The committee is electing a new chairperson today. After much discussion, Grandmother Chen is elected chairperson.

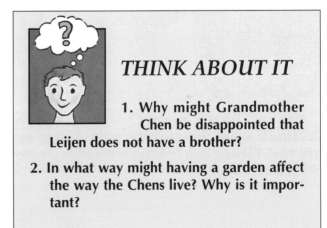

THINK ABOUT IT

1. Why might Grandmother Chen be disappointed that Leijen does not have a brother?

2. In what way might having a garden affect the way the Chens live? Why is it important?

Mr. Chen Zhongxing (Father)

As a young boy, Chen Zhongxing (Grandmother Chen's son) used to follow his father to the hills to gather Chinese herbs for medicine. Sometimes he would watch his father tend to his patients. His father wanted him to have a Western education, and to become a doctor. Zhongxing was a bright student. He attended a missionary school, and later went on to university. He became interested in physics, and taught it at university.

During the **Cultural Revolution** (1966-1976), Mr. Chen was sent to work in the fields. He spent 10 years there. This was where he met his wife, Shaolin. They married when the Cultural Revolution was over. Zhongxing got his job back at the university, conducting lab classes. But he felt that he had been away from physics too long. He wrote to his sisters in Canada to ask them to send him up-to-date books on physics.

Mr. Chen Speaks

Every day I ride my bicycle to and from work. By the time I get home, I am usually tired. But every day after work, I study until midnight. I study in the bedroom. No one may disturb my work. I am also trying to learn English. I hope to go to Canada to study. I would like to see my sisters there. This has been my dream for several years.

Like many Chinese citizens, Chen Zhongxing rides his bicycle to and from work every day. Bicycles are practical. They are easy to take care of and do not cost much to keep up.

Mrs. Chen, Wu Shaolin (Mother)

When Shaolin met Zhongxing, she was a young student. She was sent to the fields to help educate the peasants. After long days of work, Zhongxing would invite Shaolin to chat and to teach her about Chinese medicine. When they decided to marry, Grandmother Chen was not too pleased. She felt that Shaolin was not good enough for her son. After all, Shaolin only finished junior middle school, and she was a Red Guard during the Cultural Revolution. Red Guards were known for destroying the old to build the new.

Zhongxing and Shaolin finally married. They lived together with Grandmother Chen in the family home. Shaolin tried her best to please her mother-in-law, but felt that she did not succeed. When Leijen was born, Grandmother Chen told Shaolin that she had not fulfilled her duty as a daughter-in-law because she had not had a son. Shaolin and her husband had discussed their family plans. They wished to follow the One Child policy of the country. They would only have one child because they knew that China already had so many people.

After work, Shaolin likes to read the People's Daily *newspaper.*

Mrs. Chen Speaks

After I had my daughter, I decided to go back to work. I was glad when I found a job at a day-care just 5 km from our home. Each day I work from 6:30 in the morning until 6:30 in the evening. It takes me 40 minutes on the bus to get to work. During my lunch break, I go to the nearby market to shop for our daily groceries. Sometimes on my way home, I try to get fresh milk and fruit for Leijen. On the bus home, if I am lucky enough to get a seat, I like to read the People's Daily. *By the time I get back to the apartment, dinner is all prepared by Grandmother Chen. I do the dishes after dinner. Then, I help my daughter, usually for one hour, to review her homework.*

In the evenings, the women in the family sit down and watch television. Sometimes, I sew while I watch. These days, Leijen does not want home-sewn clothes. I sew for other people to earn money to buy luxury items for the family. I would like to save money for a

THINK ABOUT IT

1. **Why does Shaolin think of a washing machine as a luxury item? Do you think it is a luxury? Why?**

2. **Why do you think Zhongxing changed tradition and did not marry someone his mother approved of?**

washing machine. This will probably take me several years. Zhongxing's savings are going toward his studies overseas. I am not looking forward to my husband leaving to study. I will be alone with Grandmother Chen. Fortunately, my Leijen will be here with me.

Chen Leijen (Daughter)

Leijen has been raised by her grandmother. Ever since she was young, she could remember her grandmother singing to her.

She feels that she is very fortunate being the only child in the family. She is close to her mother, but they do not have much time to spend together, except on Sundays. This is when father, mother, and daughter go to the park in the morning. Then they go home to fetch grandmother to take her to the restaurant close by for dimsum, a Chinese lunch. Afterward, they will sit along the bank of the Zhujiang for an hour before walking home.

Leijen is very proud to have aunties and cousins in Canada. On her birthday and at New Year she receives nice gifts from them. These are usually very stylish clothes and toys. Lately they have sent her some storybooks in English, with cassette tapes to go with them. Her two aunties brought the colour tv and the radio-cassette player with them when they visited China three years ago. Leijen has brought many friends to her home to show them her prized possessions.

THINK ABOUT IT

1. Does Leijen think of the colour tv and the radio-cassette player as luxury items? How can you tell?

2. The Chens try hard to spend time together as a family. How important do you think shared family time is?

Leijen is a student of Gucheng Second Elementary School. There, she studies Chinese, mathematics, politics, science, painting, music, crafts, and gym. She is in her sixth year of school. This year, at her school, she will begin to learn English. Leijen has already learned to speak some English from her father. She would like to learn more so that one day she can talk to her Canadian cousins, who do not speak Chinese!

Leijen walks to school after eating a breakfast of rice porridge and a steamed bun.

Leijen Speaks

On weekday mornings, I wake up at 7:00 AM and spend half an hour washing and getting dressed for school. Usually, grandmother prepares my breakfast. I eat rice porridge and a steamed bun with meat. After breakfast, I walk to school, which takes me 5 minutes. From the time I reach school until 8:00 AM, I read.

My first class is mathematics, followed by Chinese or politics. From 9:45 to 10:00 there is exercise for everyone. My third class is science or gym, followed by painting or music. From 11:40 to 12 noon, I stay in school for lunch. Everyone is served the same meal. Usually, it consists of some meat, vegetables, and rice.

After lunch, we have free time, when we can play outside, or inside when it rains. Afternoon classes start at 1:00 with crafts or science. My sixth class is painting or politics. Seventh class is revision, when everyone reviews all that they have learned in the day. Then we have homework assignments. After assembly at 4:00, we are ready to go home. When I get home from school, I usually have a snack. Then I work on my homework until 6:00. I watch tv until mother comes home from work. After supper, mother and I review my homework for an hour. Then we sit down to watch tv together.

At 9:00 I practise the violin for half an hour. Then I go to bed.

THINK ABOUT IT

1. **In your notebook, make two schedules of a weekday routine, beginning with waking up. Make one schedule for yourself and one for Leijen. Are your schedules alike? How are they different?**

2. **When you are sitting in class, do you sometimes think about the other children your age doing the same thing? Write a letter to an imaginary student in China. Tell her or him what you think about daily life in China as it is described in this chapter. Tell the student why you think it would be good for students in Canada and China to know more about each other.**

On Sundays, the Chens spend time together as a family. After lunch, they go for a walk along the Zhujiang.

A LOOK BACK

In this chapter, you learned about the daily lives of the Chen family, an ordinary family in China. You read about how the Chens meet their basic needs. You also learned about how the relationship between China and Canada can be important to the people living in China.

The Chen family is balancing traditional and modern beliefs every day. Their daily lives show how important ancestors and older family members are to modern Chinese families. Celebrating through festivals allows the Chens to do things as a family while keeping traditions alive. Honouring traditions allows the Chens to live in harmony with each other.

The conflict between modern and traditional beliefs is also present in the Chens' daily lives. The changing role of women and the practice of having only one child can cause older family members to question modern ways. Younger family members are able to see how China has changed and is changing, so they follow different practices. Conflict between family members in China can occur, then, because younger people want to change more quickly than older family members. Older members sometimes do not understand the need for change because traditional ways have worked well for them. Like in our families, older and younger people in China eventually find a balance between traditional and modern practices. Even though the Chens do not always agree, they still live in relative harmony with each other.

The Chens' relationship with their Canadian relatives demonstrates how sharing goods can help improve lifestyles. Chinese families want luxury items like televisions and radio-cassette players, but these goods are very expensive in China. Because the same goods are much less expensive in Canada, the Chens' Canadian relatives buy them in Canada and take them to China. The Chens enjoy more luxury items through the sharing relationship with Canadian relatives.

Mr. Chen's desire for Canadian education in physics demonstrates that knowledge can be shared between Chinese and Canadian people. The attention Leijen gives to her studies also shows how important education is to Chinese people.

A LOOK AHEAD

- In the next chapter, you will learn more about schools. Do you think Chinese schools are much different from Canadian ones? Read on and find out!
- Schools in China have changed over the years. At one time, only certain people could go to school.
- Education is very important in China. Students who learn new ideas may try to change the way things are.

Questions

1. Look back to the Chapter Focus questions. Answer these questions in your notebook.
2. Each member of the Chen family has an individual story. Which character do you find the most interesting? Why?
3. Describe the roles of each Chen family member and how these roles help the Chens meet their needs. For example, what would happen if Grandmother Chen did not help Mr. and Mrs. Chen?
4. Review the ways in which Eileen Chu in chapter 1 and Mrs. Lam in chapter 6 described their lives as little girls in China. In one paragraph, discuss the ways in which Leijen's experiences as a young girl in China are the same as Eileen's and Mrs. Lam's. In a second paragraph, tell how Leijen's experiences are different. In a third paragraph, identify which person you would most like to have the same experiences as, and give at least three reasons for your choice.

Activities

1. Compare your family with the Chen family. What are the similarities? What are the differences?
2. If you were to live a day in China, how do you think you would spend that day? What are the things you would do and not do?

CHAPTER 8

Education

Gold has a price, but

Learning is priceless

—*Old Chinese Saying*

CHAPTER FOCUS

You will read about schools in China, and how they have changed over time. As you read, think about the role of education in making changes to the Chinese way of life. Try to answer these questions:

- How have Chinese schools changed over time?

- How are modern China's schools helping the Chinese people meet their needs for a better lifestyle?

- How is China's education system linked to the government's goals for the Chinese people?

THINK ABOUT IT

1. With a partner, brainstorm ideas about schools and how they help people meet their needs.

2. With a partner, make a list of goals which you think schools try to meet. Discuss your answers to #1 and #2 with the class.

FOOD FOR THOUGHT

What food helps you study? The Chinese have a story about the kind of food that helps you study for hours! It is called *Crossing-the-Bridge Noodles*.

A young man was studying hard for examinations. To concentrate harder, he left his wife and moved into a small, quiet house across the river. His wife was worried about her husband. She wanted to give him a hot lunch every day.

Every day she crossed the bridge with his lunch. Every day the lunch got cold. One day, she had an idea. She poured hot noodles and soup into a large bowl, then poured enough hot vegetable oil on top to cover the soup. The oil held in the heat.

When she arrived at her husband's house, the noodles were still hot! The dish became famous as *Crossing-the-Bridge-Noodles*, a dish for students who study long hours!

Crossing-the-Bridge-Noodles is made of noodles, soup, and hot vegetable oil. The oil keeps the soup hot.

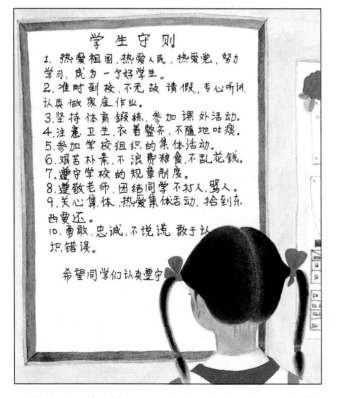

Leijen's school has many rules. Leijen is expected to remember and follow them.

Are Rules Important?

In chapter 7, you saw how Leijen spends a typical day in school. Leijen's school has rules:

Rules of Conduct

1. Love the motherland, the people, and the Communist Party of China. Study hard and be a good student.

2. Come to school on time and do not be absent from class without a good reason. Listen closely and complete all homework.

3. Persist in physical exercise and participate in extracurricular activities.

4. Stress hygiene, keep clothes tidy and clean. Do not spit.

5. Love physical labour and do for yourself whatever you are able to do on your own.

6. Live plainly, consume grain economically. Do not be fussy about food and clothes, and do not squander money.

7. Abide by school discipline and public order.

8. Respect teachers, be united with schoolmates, be polite to others, don't scold or fight with others.

9. Be concerned about the group, love public property, and turn in things you find.

10. Be brave and honest. Do not tell lies. Correct your own mistakes.

THINK ABOUT IT

1. **What are the rules at your school? Why do you think rules are important?**

2. **Compare your school rules to Leijen's school rules. What do school rules tell us about Chinese and Canadian lifestyles?**

These students attend elementary school in China. Their school day consists of study, exercise, and activities.

School in Modern China

From a very early age, children in China are taught that education is important. They go to school six days a week, and they usually have homework every night. Everyone is concerned about the education of the nation's children.

In China today, whether you are rich or poor, a boy or a girl, you may go to school. Students go to playschool, elementary school, and middle school. Parents pay a small tuition fee. From ages three to six, children can attend playschool while their parents work. These playschools are like Canadian day-care centres. Activities help children learn to get along with one another.

From ages seven to eleven, children attend elementary school. Children learn to speak their country's official language, Putonghua. The school day consists of study, exercise, and activities. Approximately 65 per cent of the children will finish elementary school; others quit school to work. After elementary school, children enter middle school.

Middle school is divided into junior middle and senior middle years, like junior and senior high in Canada. There are three years each at the junior and senior levels. Students must pass an entrance examination to get into senior middle school.

After middle school, students may go to university. To enter university, students must pass another exam. Only 5 per cent will be accepted. The rest have to find a job. Those who go to university are the **elite**, or most favoured, in China.

Schooling in China starts at an early age. Today, day-care centres are as important in China as they are in Canada.

A Modern Classroom in China

A Teacher Speaks

I am Wu Shaomei. I teach language in Guangzhou No. 7 Elementary School. I teach third year elementary students. I have 48 students. Most are just learning our official language, Putonghua. When they start school, I use Guangdonghua (Cantonese) to teach them. Slowly, I introduce Putonghua.

I teach the different sounds and tones. I talk most of the time in Putonghua. When they don't understand, I explain in their dialect. Slowly, they learn to speak in simple sentences. I wish their parents would speak more Putonghua at home so they could practise.

I give lots of homework every day. Students practise writing Chinese characters, and learn poems and songs by ear. If they do not complete their homework, I stay after school with them. They need to study hard to learn our language well.

To me, teaching is an important career. It helps the young people of our country become good citizens.

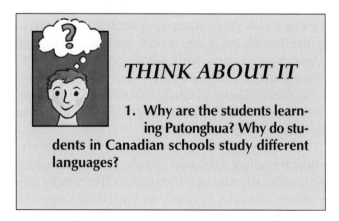

THINK ABOUT IT

1. Why are the students learning Putonghua? Why do students in Canadian schools study different languages?

How Has School in China Changed?

At one time, going to school in China was a great privilege. Only a few men were allowed to go. In ancient China, the most intelligent and well educated men were selected to be **civil servants** who helped govern the country. Before 1949, only two out of every ten people could read or write.

To be selected as civil servants, young men had to study Chinese history and literature with famous scholars, and take many tests. This process took years. Some talented students from poor families were sponsored by wealthy people, but usually it was only the men from rich families who could afford this education. The old Chinese system for selecting civil service candidates was later adopted by European countries.

In the Confucian system, women were not educated because they were considered inferior. Sons from the merchant class were also left out because merchants were not highly regarded. The common people remained **illiterate**. The educated class was held in the highest respect. Education was a privilege few could enjoy.

As you read earlier, education is now available to all the people of China. Schools and education have changed a great deal in China over the years.

RESEARCH

1. **Interview a senior person in your community. Talk to** him or her about the time he or she went to school. Ask the senior what school was like. What did he or she have to learn in school? What were the school rules? What was most important to him or her about school?

2. **After you have done your interview, write down the similarities and differences between schools in the old days and today. Get together in small groups to talk about your findings.**

THE EARLIEST CALCULATOR

The abacus was first developed by the Chinese hundreds of years ago. It is a hand calculator for addition, subtraction, division, and multiplication. In the hands of a skilled user, it can be faster than an electronic calculator! Chinese children are sometimes taught the basic techniques of the abacus in school. In some Chinatowns in Canada, you might see them used by storekeepers.

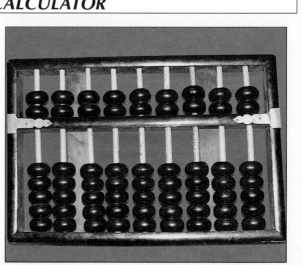

The abacus was invented centuries ago. It is used to work out simple math problems.

Missionaries from Canada built some of the first Chinese schools that allowed both boys and girls to study. Today, students from Canada and China come together in events like this gymnastics competition.

Missionaries Influence Change in Chinese Schools

In the early 1800s, Western Christian missionaries built many schools in China. They taught Western science and **economics**. Many of these schools allowed both boys and girls to study. This was something new and revolutionary!

Canadian missionaries built some of these schools. They played an important role in establishing some of China's universities. Canadian, British, and American missionaries built the West China Union College in Chengdu, Sichuan province, in 1910. This university is now called the Sichuan Medical University.

Government Makes Further Changes to China's Schools

The Chinese government learned from the successes of girls in missionary schools. It decided to allow girls to attend all schools. Through contact with other nations, China's government also decided that the only way for China to modernize was to educate its people. To do this, education was made available to all people—rich or poor, country or city-dwellers.

As in Canadian schools, good citizenship was one of the goals of public education in China. Students were taught about government policies and learned how good citizens behave. The government wanted citizens who would work together to make China stronger. Students were taught to put the country's goals ahead of their personal goals.

A big difference between China's and Canada's schools was most noticeable during a period called the Cultural Revolution of 1966-1976. (In chapter 11, you will read more about the Cultural Revolution and Mao Zedong, China's leader at that time.) The government during this time thought education should include manual labour. Students like Mr. Chen were forced to work on farms. The belief was that by working with the peasants, students would better understand the lifestyles of country people in China. As you have read, this practice interrupted the education of many people. Like Mr. Chen, they had to begin their studies again, years later. China lost many valuable years of educational time because of this policy.

Eventually, government thinking changed again. Students were no longer sent to work on farms. They competed for high marks. Again, they had to write exams to get into university. Students were encouraged to learn foreign languages, and some students were allowed to study in foreign countries. The government was less involved in schools after 1976.

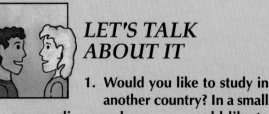

LET'S TALK ABOUT IT

1. Would you like to study in another country? In a small group, discuss where you would like to study and why. What would it feel like to study in another country? How would you benefit from such an experience?

Students demonstrated for more freedom in Tiananmen Square in Beijing. Their banner read, "Long live the students!" The students stood up to the forces of the government.

Students Organize to Bring Change

In 1987, the Chinese government had to pay close attention to the actions of students. Many of China's students were openly questioning whether China's system of government was a good one. As a result, the government placed more controls on university students who were studying **abroad**. Even with these controls, ideas about **democracy** and freedom became popular among Chinese students.

The government's tougher policies did not stop the protests. Students and workers wanted more freedom. In 1989, a demonstration with thousands of people took place in Tiananmen Square, in Beijing. The demonstration ended in a massacre of protesters by Chinese armed forces, who came with guns and tanks.

The government then forced even more rules on the people. Students were expected to study hard to make China a strong nation. They were not allowed to criticize the government. Many students are now expected to work on farms again.

Several students left China or took **refuge** in countries where they were studying. This event was one which focussed attention on China. China's government is still reacting to it.

THINK ABOUT IT

1. Going to school is one way to learn about our world. How does education help you meet your needs now? How might education help you in the future?

2. Why might Western ideas be unpopular with China's government? (Hint: Think about the way in which China's government wants personal goals to come second to the nation's goals.)

A LOOK BACK

China's educational system has changed over time. Modern schools play a large role in China's goals for the future, because China's moves to modernize need a well educated population.

In the past, only a few people, usually the sons of wealthy families, had access to education. Because of Confucianism, women were not allowed to go to school. The limits placed on who could go to school meant that very few Chinese people could even read or write.

As China came into contact with other countries and their beliefs, education changed. Western Christian missionaries were some of the first to help change China's education system. The new ideas brought by foreigners were sometimes viewed as bad ideas. During the Cultural Revolution, the government sent Chinese teachers and students to the country to humble them, and remind them they were not better than farm workers. Most recently, students in Beijing's Tiananmen Square were punished with physical violence when they challenged China's government to pursue democracy.

Even though education is now open to all who want it, the government still controls the ideas students learn. The goal of the Chinese government to produce good citizens may yet be opposed by the students who are seeking change in government.

A LOOK AHEAD

- In the next chapter, you will read about farming in China. China's farmers grow different kinds of food and use different methods to do so.

- A common greeting in China is "Have you eaten?" In the next chapter, you will find out why.

- The lifestyles of China's farmers are changing. The next chapter tells you about these changes and gives you a chance to think about changes in Canada also.

Questions

1. With a partner, discuss the Chapter Focus questions. Record your answers to these questions in your notebook.

2. In China, education has always been highly valued. Why?

3. In Chinese schools, some subjects are considered very important. What are they? Discuss why they are so important.

4. Educational opportunities are different from country to country. What are the differences and similarities in educational opportunities in China and in Canada?

Activities

1. Using magazines and encyclopedias, research the Tiananmen Square massacre. Write a report about why you think Chinese students behaved as they did. What needs were the students trying to meet? Skim back through this text to review the ways in which Chinese students have been involved in making change. Record major actions of students in your notebook.

2. Review the rules for Leijen's school earlier in this chapter. Identify, in a paragraph, which rules you would find the most difficult to follow and explain why. Describe which of your needs might not be met if you followed all the rules outlined.

CHAPTER 9

Agriculture

When eating bamboo shoots

Remember who planted them

—*Old Chinese Saying*

CHAPTER FOCUS

You will read about China's system of agriculture and how ways of farming have changed in China over time. As you read, think about how China's agricultural system has changed to meet the needs of the country's large population. Try to answer the following questions:

- How has modern agricultural **technology** changed the ways Chinese meet their need for food?

- What kinds of crops are grown in China?

- How has the Chinese government affected the way food is grown and distributed?

THINK ABOUT IT

1. How does your family meet its need for food? Do you grow a garden? Do you or your friends have a farm?

2. Visit a grocery store. Try to identify foods which are grown in Canada. List these. Next, identify at least five foods which are not grown in Canada. Ask store personnel how the foods came to your country. Record your findings.

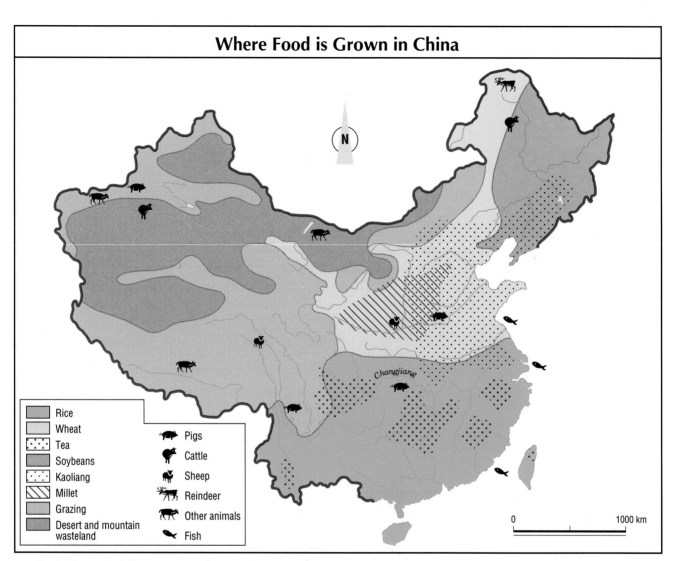

Where Food is Grown in China

Rice
Wheat
Tea
Soybeans
Kaoliang
Millet
Grazing
Desert and mountain wasteland

Pigs
Cattle
Sheep
Reindeer
Other animals
Fish

Changjiang

0   1000 km

Agriculture is different in northern and southern China. Can you explain the differences?

Food in China

Food in China is as varied as its peoples and languages. As the Changjiang divides China into north and south, it also divides Chinese cuisine into northern and southern styles.

The main food of northern China is wheat, made into bread and noodles. The southern people depend mainly on rice. Ancestors of the southern people were the first Chinese to immigrate to North America. This made North Americans think that because these Chinese ate rice, all Chinese ate rice!

The Chinese eat all kinds of meat, poultry, fish, eggs, and grains. Like Canadians, the Chinese have a diet that includes items from all food groups.

Rice Farming

Rice farming is a little different from farming other cereal grains. Rice fields are called *paddies*. They need special preparation. Because the field must be flooded with water before the seedlings can be planted, a small bank is built around the field. This bank holds in the water.

The seedlings are grown in seed trays for about three weeks. Then, each seedling is planted by hand into a hole which is underwater. When the rice has grown between 60 and 180 cm, and has a full head of seeds, it is time to drain the water out of the paddy and bring in the harvest.

Rice is a member of the grass family. About half the people in the world eat rice every day.

Growing rice is different from growing other cereal crops. The paddy is flooded, and the seedlings are planted under water.

"Have You Eaten?"

China has a population of over 1 billion people. It has one quarter of the world's population. China is faced with the challenge of feeding all these people every day. This is an enormous task for Chinese farmers, who have only 7 per cent of the world's **arable** land.

Because food is so important, a common greeting among the Chinese around mealtimes is "Have you eaten?" instead of "How are you?"

To the Chinese, rich or poor, food is to be enjoyed individually and with friends and family. Often, meals are occasions for special celebrations, such as festivals, weddings, births, funerals, and family and social gatherings.

HOW ARE CROPS IN CHINA LIKE CANADIAN CROPS?

Canadian crops are similar to crops grown in northern China. In that region of China, the growing season is short, as it is in most of Canada. The main crops are wheat, corn, potatoes, and sugarbeets.

South of the Great Wall, the climate is milder. The farther south you travel in China, the milder the climate becomes. In southern China, crops that grow well are tobacco, peanuts, and cotton. Farmers also grow tea and mulberry. Mulberry leaves are used to feed silkworms. These crops do not grow well in Canada's climate.

Some rice is grown in northern China, but most rice is grown in the warmer, wetter south. Because rice needs plenty of water to grow, the farmers build elaborate **irrigation** systems. Some Canadian farmers use irrigation, too, but Canada's climate is not suitable to grow rice.

For the Chinese, many celebrations happen around the dinner table.

Apples and pears are common fruits in China. They are harvested in the autumn.

Common Livestock and Fruit Crops in China

In both northern and southern China, pigs, chickens, and cattle are the most common farm animals. Farmers sell most of their animals to buyers from the government. The government then packages and sells meats to the people. Some farm animals are brought to open public markets. There, they are either sold directly to interested buyers, or they are traded to other farmers for things like wheat and rice.

Fresh fruits are an important part of China's farm production. Most fruits are grown in the south. Apples, pears, peaches, and oranges are the most common fruits grown.

What Foods Do the Chinese Eat, and How Do They Eat?

The most common food in southern China is rice. It is usually combined with vegetables, meat, or fish. In northern China, the most common dish is a type of flour dumpling with a meat or vegetable filling inside. There are very few foods that are "especially for children" in China. Youngsters are expected to eat the same foods as adults.

Almost everyone in China eats with chopsticks. These eating utensils may be made of wood, ivory, plastic, or bamboo. They are used with a bowl, rather than a plate. The bowl is picked up and held close to the mouth. To use chopsticks, move one stick toward the other so you can pick up food between the sticks. Many people in other countries, including Korea, Japan, Thailand—and Canada— also use chopsticks.

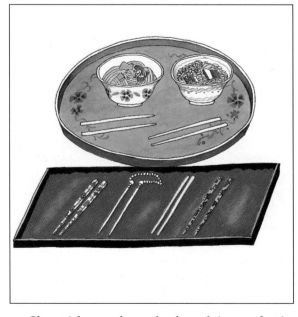

Chopsticks may be made of wood, ivory, plastic, or bamboo.

In China, much of the farm labour is still done by humans and animals.

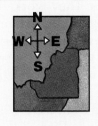

READING MAPS

1. **Look at the maps on pages 29 and 76.**

   (a) **Locate the areas where wheat and millet are grown in China.**

   (b) **Locate the areas where rice, tea, and soybeans are grown.**

2. **Why do you think these crops grow where they do?**

What Were China's Traditional Ways of Farming?

Farming started in China 6000 years ago! People started to irrigate along the Huang River to grow rice. Rice was introduced into China from India. It was first grown along the Changjiang valley, in the wetlands. The technique of transplanting rice seedlings into rice paddies was used long ago, and is still used today.

Farming in ancient China was back-breaking work that the whole family had to help with. Everything was done by hand, except ploughing was sometimes done by animals such as water buffalo or oxen.

Water buffalo have been and still are a part of farming in China. These strong animals have a thick hide, but in the hot sun, the hide can crack. To stay healthy, they must soak in water twice each day. It is usually the children's job to take the family's buffalo for its bath.

How Did Communes Change Farm Work?

In the past, farming anywhere in the world was often difficult. The hours were sun-up to sun-down. Months of hard work could be ruined by windstorms, drought, or other natural events. Even today, making a living by farming is not easy.

Historically, the way Chinese farming was organized also made farming difficult. Before the Communists came to power in 1949, farmland was owned by rich people. Peasant farmers worked on the land, but they did not own it. As a result, they paid high rents to the landlord just to work on the land. The rents were so high that the peasants had a hard time providing enough food and clothing for their families.

When Mao Zedong and the Communists took power in 1949, they made many changes to the way land was farmed. One big change was to take the land away from the rich landlords and give it to the farmers. By 1952, most farmland was owned by peasants.

The Communist Party then made peasants work together. It asked them to share human power and machinery. In 1958, the Communists joined huge chunks of land to form **communes**.

Communes had small factories and workshops to repair farm equipment. These factories also made fertilizer, steel, small machinery, cement, and processed food.

People lived on the communes. They worked together and shared the things they needed to live. Everyone was supposed to be treated equally under the commune system, whatever work he or she did. The government controlled what happened to things the communes made.

The commune system was used from the 1950s to the 1970s. Each commune provided for all the needs of the people living in the commune.

In the 1960s, many Canadian farmers went to China to learn how Chinese farms worked. They were impressed by the cooperation and sharing of labour and machinery. Many Canadians already knew about cooperative farming because some Canadians, like the Hutterites, farm that way.

After Communes, What Next?

The commune system did not work according to plan. It did succeed at meeting the basic needs of the people, such as food, health care, and education. It also provided families with a guaranteed living. But, the system did not give people the wish to produce more than what was required. Some people did not feel it was a fair system. They did not like the fact that everything was shared equally. People who worked hard received no more than people who did not.

It was several years until a new system took its place. After Chairman Mao died in 1976, the commune system was dropped. New ways of organizing production were started. The new system that was put into place was called the Responsibility System.

Under this system, Chinese farmers have a responsibility to produce a set amount (a **quota**) to sell to the government. If the farmer can produce more than the quota, he or she can sell the extra products at a market and keep the money. There are many markets in the countryside now, selling fresh produce and livestock.

The Responsibility System, with the help of more modern machinery, irrigation canals and dams, and natural and chemical pesticides, provides peasants with more security for their crops. Before, there was little money for technological improvement. Now, modern farming is becoming an important area of research and production in China.

Irrigation canals, like this one, ensure that farmers' fields get plenty of water.

THINK ABOUT IT

1. After reading the dialogue on page 81, make a chart listing the similarities and differences between the commune system and the Responsibility System. Write a paragraph about which system best meets China's need to produce food.

Two Farmers Talk About the Responsibility System

In the following conversation, two Chinese farmers compare the commune system to the Responsibility System.

Wang: *The commune system was not as bad as some people say. At least, it guaranteed prices and incomes.*

Jia: *Yes, but everybody received the same pay, no matter how hard they worked—or didn't work. Some people were lazy.*

Wang: *But now, with the Responsibility System, everyone has to grow extra crops. Everyone spends their spare time selling products in the market. We have to work extra hard to make ends meet.*

Jia: *The extra work is worth it. Now we have washing machines, television sets, and we can afford to take a holiday now and then. Some people have built new homes. Some have their own farm machines, such as tractors and trucks.*

Wang: *Not everyone lives so well. Many people cannot keep up. There are more poor people these days.*

Jia: *Yes, but everyone was poor before. I like it better now. If I want to work harder, I can earn more. It is up to me.*

Wang: *Before, everything was orderly and regulated. We decided together which crops to grow. Now, people plant only the crops that make the most money. There is too much of one crop and not enough of others. There is no planning.*

Jia: *China is a very big place! There is always a market for extra crops. Besides, not every region grows the same things. Now, there is more trade among regions.*

Wang: *Before, the communes produced **surplus** products to benefit China. New industries could be built with the money from selling these products. These days people are more selfish. They use the surplus products to get rich. They think more of themselves than of China.*

Jia: *I suppose we will never agree. We will just have to agree to disagree. But that is better than before. In the past, no one was allowed to be different.*

Wang: *That's true. Perhaps none of us has all the answers.*

Technology Changes China's Farming Methods

In China, 80 per cent of the people live in rural areas and depend on farming for their living, but only 15 per cent of China's land is suitable for farming. As a result, it is important for the Chinese to make use of their land in the most productive way.

Since the 1980s, China has tried to find modern ways to farm. Chinese scientists look for new ways of developing seeds and growing crops. Some modern farm machines, such as the tractor, have been introduced. Modern and traditional farming methods are used to till the soil, sow the seeds, and reap the harvest.

Instead of putting all of their energy into growing grains, the Chinese do many kinds of farming. Tree farming, fish farming, and raising animals are all common in China. With the help of other countries, China is trying to become a nation that can feed all of its people.

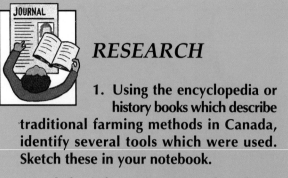

RESEARCH

1. Using the encyclopedia or history books which describe traditional farming methods in Canada, identify several tools which were used. Sketch these in your notebook.

2. Search for information on modern farming methods in Canada. What changes have been made in the tools used? Why have these changes been necessary?

New farming technology, like this tractor used in rice farming, helps China make productive use of its land.

TECHNOLOGY, FARMING, AND PEOPLE: THE THREE GORGES DAM PROJECT

In the 1990s, China's government decided that it needed to create more electricity to power the country's factories. It chose to build a huge series of dams, called the Three Gorges Dam project. These dams would be the biggest building project in China since the construction of the Great Wall! When completed, they would generate large amounts of electricity.

But many people in China—and elsewhere in the world—fear that the dams will have other effects. The dams will destroy large amounts of farmland, forcing a million people off their land. There are also worries that China's climate could be changed by the Three Gorges project. Climate changes would also have an impact on Chinese agriculture. The Three Gorges project is a good example of the effect technology can have on farming and on people's lives.

China is not the only country whose need for a great deal of energy can cause serious problems. The Three Gorges Dam project will sacrifice farmland and homes for electricity. Likewise, in Canada, the James Bay Project in Quebec has sparked much controversy. The Quebec government wants to build huge dams to generate electricity. Environmentalists and Native groups worry that the dams will harm North America's environment, and destroy people's homes. It is not always easy to meet everyone's needs in a fair and balanced way!

LET'S TALK ABOUT IT

1. **Do you think governments should build large projects like the Three Gorges dams without thinking about all the consequences these projects might have?**

2. **What are some other reasons for huge projects like Three Gorges or James Bay? Can you think of other ways of meeting people's need for energy?**

A LOOK BACK

Agriculture is a very important industry in China. Because of China's large population and limited arable land, the Chinese people are always exploring new ways of farming.

Traditionally, China's land was controlled by rich landowners. Peasants rented the land. The work was very hard, required many labourers, and barely allowed the Chinese farmers to meet their basic needs. Changes were made to this farming system when the Communist government came to power in 1949.

The Communist Party tried two ways of organizing farming—the commune system and the Responsibility System. The commune system put group needs ahead of individual needs. It was reasonably successful in helping Chinese farmers meet their basic needs. This system failed, however, to allow farmers to meet their need to be rewarded according to individual effort. It also did little to make farming less difficult work than in the past.

The latest system, the Responsibility System, has promoted the addition of new technology to Chinese farming. Research into better methods of farming plus more modern tools allow farmers in China to produce more with less effort. When less effort is required to meet the government quotas, individual farmers can produce surplus goods for personal profit. All of these changes are helping today's Chinese farmers improve their lifestyles.

Changes to China's agricultural industry will continue to be made. Technology and growing trade relationships with countries like Canada will help farmers meet the country's need for food and to improve their personal lifestyles. As with Canadian farming, technology and trade may allow the Chinese to spend less time on agriculture and more on developing other industries. In the future, China may be able to use agricultural land for other purposes, such as the Three Gorges Dam project.

Whatever changes are made in China, however, the farmers will continue to grow a variety of crops to satisfy their country's need for food. It may be some time before the greeting "Have you eaten?" becomes less important to the Chinese.

A LOOK AHEAD

- In the next chapter, you will read about China's growth in science and technology. As you will read, Canada has played a role in sharing its technology with China.

- China's inventions have impressed people the world over. Gunpowder and paper are two examples of Chinese inventions.

- Chinese medicine and health care are a blend of traditional and modern practices.

- Many forms of transportation are used in China.

Questions

1. Answer the Chapter Focus questions in your notebook.

2. Technology has come slowly to the rice fields of China. From this chapter, and from further research in an encyclopedia, write a paragraph to describe how rice is planted, tended, and harvested in China. Has there been much change to date? What changes did you find?

3. Irrigation is an important part of rice farming. What crops do Canadian farmers irrigate? Use an atlas to help you answer.

4. What changes have been made to Chinese farming methods in the past 100 years? Identify these changes on a chart according to major and minor change. In a paragraph, discuss how these changes have affected the ways in which Chinese farmers meet their needs.

Activities

1. Like the Chinese, Canadian farmers are changing the way they do things as new technologies and information become available. Research the changes in farming technology over the past few years in areas such as machinery, crops, or planting and harvesting techniques.

   (a) What general trends have resulted as these are introduced? Discuss these changes in a paragraph. (HINT: You may want to examine farm size, numbers of people working in agriculture, and crops grown.)

   (b) In a second paragraph, describe how these changes affect farmers and other Canadians' lifestyles.

CHAPTER 10

Technologies

Preserve the old

But know the new

—*Old Chinese Saying*

CHAPTER FOCUS

In this chapter, you will read about some Chinese inventions and technologies that are used all over the world. As you read, think about how changes in science, communication, and transportation have helped the Chinese to meet their needs for health care, transportation, and communication. Try to answer the following questions:

- How did the Chinese belief in harmony affect the use of technologies?

- What are some of the Chinese inventions that are shared with other countries?

- How have changes in science, communication, and transportation helped the Chinese to become more modern?

- Why are the Chinese exploring ways of improving science, communication, and transportation methods in China?

THINK ABOUT IT

1. Think of some recent inventions, for example, tv, cd players, or rollerblade skates. How have these inventions affected the way you live? What would your life be like if these things had never been invented?

Firecrackers are now a part of celebrations throughout the world.

Science: Chinese Inventions

You have read that the ancient Chinese believed humans should live in harmony with nature. This belief affected the way Chinese scientists pursued their studies. They believed that nature was governed by a set of laws. They believed people had to live within these laws and that human inventions should not harm nature.

The Chinese used their discoveries carefully. They did not try to conquer nature. They tried to find better ways to live and work *with* nature.

Many Chinese inventions are famous in many parts of the world. Some of the most well-known inventions and discoveries are gunpowder, paper-making, printing with movable type, and the compass. Many of these inventions were used in peaceful ways.

Gunpowder was used to make firecrackers. Paper was used to print works of literature for Chinese scholars to read. The compass and new ships helped to improve Chinese trade. Because the Chinese believed their ideas were the best in the world, they concentrated on using their inventions in their own land.

Europeans were eager to use Chinese inventions, but they used them in different ways than the Chinese. Gunpowder made it easier for one kingdom to fight and conquer another. Printing and paper allowed the people of Europe to learn more about the world. Europeans used the compass to explore the globe and claim new lands.

The same inventions that the Chinese used at home helped Europeans to explore the world. By the 1800s, Europeans had invaded China several times and had helped to make it very weak!

The compass allowed Chinese navigators to sail vast distances and to find trade routes.

PAPER

What would we do without paper? We write on it, wrap, cover, buy, and carry with it. We use it so often we hardly think about it.

Scientists have found 2000-year-old paper in China. The earliest paper was made from tree bark, grass, bits of fish nets, and rags. These were boiled together, pressed, and dried. This paper had a very rough surface. Smoother paper was invented by adding rice flakes, mulberry bark, and seaweed.

The Chinese used paper not only for books, letters, and painting, but for wallpaper and paper money, too.

As paper became common, people were able to record their thoughts and share them with others. Paper has changed our lives.

We use paper to wrap, cover, buy, and carry. Paper can be made in modern factories or by hand, in the traditional way. How does paper change the way we communicate?

RESEARCH

1. **Other inventions from China are kites, wheelbarrows, spinning wheels, noodles, stirrups, crossbows, and suspension bridges. Find and record examples of how these inventions are used in Canada today.**

Traditional Chinese Medicine

The early Chinese were known for their inventions. They were also known for their medicine, which is still used in China today. Chinese-style medicine depends on three types of healing:

1. *Moxibustion* is a medical practice that is 3000 years old. It promotes healing and relief from pain by burning **tinder** over special parts of the body.

2. *Herbal medicine* uses dried roots, stems, leaves, flowers, or fungi. It also uses velvet from deer antlers, snake venom, rhinoceros horns, and animal parts. People eat or drink the medicine. Sometimes, they put it on their skin.

3. *Acupuncture* is a method of treating disease and relieving pain by putting long needles into the patient's body in special spots.

Traditionally, the Chinese believed that nature held the key to healthy living. Herbs and animal parts were often used to heal patients. The Chinese believed that good health was important.

Today, many old ways in China are changing, but the traditional views about health have changed very little. Chinese medicine has been so successful, in fact, that doctors from many Western countries now visit China to learn more about it.

RESEARCH

1. **Find the names of some plants which are used to make modern medicines. If the tropical forests where many of these plants live are destroyed, where do you think our medicines will come from in the future?**

Health Care in China and Canada

Every country has its own way of caring for the health of its people. Canadians and Chinese have the same basic idea about health care. They believe that everyone should have access to it, not just people with money.

Canadian and Chinese health care do differ in some ways. In Canada, much research is devoted to finding cures for illness. In China, much research goes into preventing illness before it can occur.

Also, in Canada, doctors are paid high salaries. In China, they are not. In Canada, most doctors have their own offices. In China, most doctors see their patients in hospitals. Only a few Chinese doctors have their own offices.

ACUPUNCTURE

Some Chinese and Western doctors use acupuncture to treat disease and control pain. They often use it with herbal medicine, and sometimes with Western medicines.

The doctor puts fine needles into the patient's body. The needles help balance the flow of energy in the patient's body. This method stops pain and helps maintain good health.

Amazingly, acupuncture does not hurt. In fact, some doctors use it instead of anesthetic when operating on patients!

Look in the phone book to see if there are acupuncturists in the place where you live.

Acupuncture involves putting long needles into the patient's body to stop pain and restore harmony. Used for centuries in China, this method is now practised in Canada.

BETHUNE, A MEDICAL FRIEND

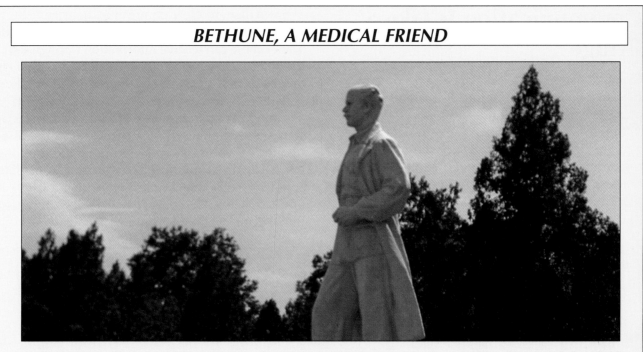

Dr. Norman Bethune trained Chinese doctors in medical work. He also cared for the wounded in field hospitals. Many Chinese remember Bethune for the work he did in their country. This statue was built to honour him.

Dr. Norman Bethune was a Canadian doctor who worked in China from 1938 to 1939. When Japan invaded China, he helped the wounded and trained the Chinese in medical work. Dr. Bethune died in China. He became a hero to many Chinese. People remember him as a symbol of international friendship. They look up to him as a man who gave his life to help the people of China. Today, he is one of the famous foreigners in recent Chinese history.

How Has China Tried to Catch Up to the West?

In the 1800s, the Chinese thought the Europeans were inferior. They called the Europeans **barbarians**. Yet, the Chinese had to admit that the Europeans were strong. You have read about how the Europeans had weakened China by the 1800s. Some Chinese believed the West was strong because of its science. The Chinese government decided to teach Western science.

The old Chinese concern about harmony with nature became less important. Many people felt the traditional ways held China back. They believed the best way to catch up with the West was to do things the Western way. They worked hard to catch up to, and even pass, the West.

In China, brick-making is done by hand. In the West, machines are usually used to make bricks.

Communication Is Like a Bridge

China is using Western science to become more modern. Better communication systems are one area they are focussing on.

In the 1920s, the Chinese government helped people learn to read. This allowed the government to communicate with its own people. This also made it easier to train people to run modern machines, and to teach young people modern subjects, such as physics, chemistry, and engineering.

Since then, modern communications have built a bridge between China and the rest of the world. The Chinese can receive information through satellite dishes. They have launched satellites with their own rockets. Movies and films are another modern way that China communicates with the world.

Canada has made many modern communication systems that China uses. Edmonton Telephones, for example, sells equipment and phone sets to China. Northern Telecom, another Canadian company, sells **switchboards** to China for hospitals and hotels. The company also sells equipment that helps transfer telephone calls.

Cities like Xi'an are centres of communication, technology, and industry.

In 1987, the Chinese made a television that can be switched from one language to another. The picture stays the same on the screen—only the language changes! Someday, Canadians may use this kind of television. Imagine how much easier it might be to learn a second, third, or fourth language!

In 1989, the students who opposed China's government at Tiananmen Square sent their message to the world using facsimile machines and cordless telephones. At the same time, the Chinese government used advanced television equipment to monitor the protesters.

All of these modern communication methods help the Chinese people to learn more about their country and the rest of the world. People in other countries have also learned more about China and its people. Communication helps people to build relationships with each other and between countries.

Transportation

Transportation in China is a mixture of old and modern methods. Because China is a large country, how to transport people and objects is an important issue.

In China, many people still move around on foot, or by bus, motorcycle, pedicab, wagon, or cart. In the country, where roads are narrow and winding, people also use donkeys, horses, or camels.

In cities and towns, electric trolley cars move many people to and from work each day. There is a modern subway system in Beijing. However, taxis and cars are not very common. Usually, only government officials or visitors use such vehicles. Private citizens are discouraged from owning vehicles because there is a lack of space to park them. The price of cars, which is much higher than in Canada, also prevents most Chinese people from owning their own cars. The most common form of transportation in China's cities is the bicycle.

The Grand Canal

The Grand Canal is an example of how the Chinese had to invent a way of moving food from one part of their vast country to another. The Chinese built it so that they could move grain from the rich Changjiang valley to the capital region of north China. The Grand Canal extends from Beijing in the north to Hangzhou in the south. This canal is more than 1700 km long. It is the longest and oldest human-made waterway in the world. It took almost 1800 years and the work of more than 5.5 million people to complete! Chinese governments wanted it built so there would be a safe route to ship grain from one part of the country to another.

The Grand Canal is about 40 m wide. In many places there are stone-paved roads on each side of it. Along the roads, trees for shade and pavilions for rest make the journey along the canal a pleasant one.

Today, diesel-powered barges and boats pass through the canal on their way north and south, carrying freight and passengers back and forth.

The old meets the new on the streets of China. Can you name the various kinds of transportation in this photograph?

A LOOK BACK

China has gone through many changes in the areas of science, communication, and transportation. Changes in these areas have helped China to modernize and build relationships with other countries.

Traditional Chinese medicine is still in use today. These practices have helped the Chinese to meet their needs for health and have been studied by many Western doctors. Modern China has a health care system very similar to Canada's. All people can have a doctor's care as they need it. Good health is important to both Chinese and Canadians.

Many Chinese inventions have been used throughout the world and have helped to change history. To understand the importance of some of these inventions, try to imagine a world without gunpowder, papermaking, printing with movable type, or compasses!

While traditional Chinese practices focussed on keeping in harmony with nature, today Chinese thinking is focussed on making China modern. Sharing knowledge and technologies with other countries like Canada, especially in the area of communication, is helping the Chinese to reach this goal. As with most things, however, change takes place over time. With such a long history and so many traditional ways still in practice, change in China is a slow process. Relationships with Western countries, however, may increase the rate of change and improve Chinese lifestyles.

An area where changes have been quite slow is transportation. A lack of space, and so many people to move from place to place, will likely continue to make transportation a big issue in China. A project like the Grand Canal is one example of how the Chinese addressed their transportation needs in the past. Making more buses, trolleys, and subways available is a way the Chinese are trying to manage their transportation needs today.

A LOOK AHEAD

- In the next chapter, we will look at how modern China is governed.

- Mao Zedong was one of China's great leaders.

- The Cultural Revolution was an important time in China's history because it brought changes to China.

- China relates to the rest of the world today.

- Government is an important part of Chinese life.

- China's government has changed over time as it tries to meet the needs of the population.

Questions

1. Answer the Chapter Focus questions in your notebook.

2. Modern ways of communicating help to change society. What are some of the changes to Chinese society?

3. In what way has scientific knowledge changed daily life in China?

4. With a partner, make a list of ways that Canadians communicate with each other and with people in other parts of the world. Discuss how these communication aids affect Canadian lifestyles. For example, imagine what life would be like without one or more of the following: radios, televisions, newspapers, telephones.

Activities

1. Take 10 minutes to look around your school. List things that the Chinese may have invented. Explain how we have adapted these things for our use. Share this in a small group.

2. How many things can you find in your own home that the Chinese invented? List them. Share your list with your family, and with your class.

CHAPTER 11

Government in Modern China

When a ruler makes a mistake

Everyone suffers

—Old Chinese Saying

CHAPTER FOCUS

As you learned in chapter 3, several changes have taken place in how the Chinese people are governed. Chapter 3 described these changes in government, from China's beginnings several thousand years ago, to 1949. In this chapter, you will read about the system of government in China from 1949 to the present. As you read, think about how China's government has tried to meet the needs of the Chinese people. Also, think about the problems facing China's government today. Try to answer the following questions:

- What are some of the major changes the Chinese government has gone through since 1949?

- What kinds of relationships has China's government had with other countries? How have the relationships changed over time?

- What problems might the Chinese government face in the future?

RESEARCH

1. Interview several adults in your community. Ask them about the ways a change in government affects them. Also, find out why a government might change. Ask them how it is decided that a change is needed. How are governments changed?

2. In your interview, ask the people what needs government helps them meet. If possible, have the people you interview rank, from most to least important, the needs which government must meet for them to be satisfied.

The Communist Government

From 1949 to Today

Mao Zedong believed that China would be a better place if it were communist.

In 1949, China changed both its name and its government. As you learned in chapter 3, the Communist Party led by Mao Zedong became China's official ruling party, and the country was renamed the People's Republic of China.

The Communist Party was very concerned with problems such as: What will help us live in peace, become modern, provide our citizens with better educations and enough food for everyone? These problems guided government policies and caused the Communists to make many changes to the way the Chinese people lived.

The Communists changed education, farming, industry, family life—and just about everything else. Guided by a belief that the old ways did not work anymore, and concerned with a rapidly growing population, the Communists made changes that affected the lives of all of China's citizens. As you have read, some of these changes worked well, while others did not. In the struggle to find new ways of solving old problems, the Communists experimented with many policies. One especially famous experiment in government policy was called the Cultural Revolution.

The Cultural Revolution

The Cultural Revolution took place in China from 1966 to 1976. For many of China's people it was a

These senior citizens have seen great changes in their lifetimes. They saw Chairman Mao introduce China to communism. In their old age, they are living through even more changes.

This poster shows enthusiastic Red Guards holding Chairman Mao's little red book, The Thoughts of Chairman Mao. *During the Cultural Revolution, everyone had to read this book.*

time when many citizens feared what their government might do next. People were told what to do and how to do it. The rules for everyone were written in a little red book called *The Thoughts of Chairman Mao.*

The main force behind the Cultural Revolution was a group called the Red Guards. Many of the Red Guards were young people who were eager to accept the new ways. In fact, China's problems persuaded the Red Guards that the old ways were bad. The Red Guards' chief aim became to destroy old ways of doing things, and bring in new ways of thinking and behaving.

Change and the Red Guards

One of the main goals of the Red Guards was to get rid of the "four olds"—old ideas, old culture, old habits, and old customs. The Red Guards used many harsh methods to achieve this goal. They burned books and discouraged people from celebrating traditional festivals. They organized young children into a group called the Little Red Guards. Children were urged to spy on their parents and report to the Red Guards if their parents behaved in "old" ways. Students were encouraged to spy on their teachers, and to report them if they did not teach "proper" Communist beliefs. Schools were closed. Parents, teachers, and anyone else who did not believe in and follow the principles of the Cultural Revolution were punished.

The Red Guards expected the people to "throw out" old ways of doing things, and to accept a great deal of change. The **intellectual class** were targeted as a group which had to be taught a new way of thinking. Many intellectuals, like Mr. Chen, were sent from China's universities to work on farms. On the farms, university students, professors, and other city workers were forced to work with their

hands. In this way, they were humbled and made to develop greater respect for the work done by farmers. The Red Guards also forced peasants to go to school and learn new ideas. Both the intellectual class and the peasants were very unhappy with the changes, but their views were not considered important. The Red Guards believed that China would only get better if all parts of society changed. This policy continued until 1976, when Mao Zedong died.

Change After Mao

In 1976, Deng Xiaoping became the new leader of the government. Under his leadership, the People's Republic of China developed stronger relationships with other countries. Chinese students were encouraged to go to foreign countries to study. Foreign countries were allowed to do more business with China. Private citizens could once again own land, open businesses, and make money for themselves.

While these changes have been quite popular in China, change has not come quickly enough for many Chinese. People have demonstrated for more freedoms and for a democratic government. Although China's government is aware that many of its citizens are unhappy, it still limits personal freedoms.

The government faces a difficult problem. On the one hand, it knows that greater freedom for China's people will be good for the country. It will mean more economic growth. On the other hand, China's leaders worry that more freedom may mean the end of the Communist Party. If people were free to choose their leaders, they might reject the party. This would put many party members, who enjoy good jobs and much power, out of work.

LET'S TALK ABOUT IT

1. **What happened when the government of China told people what to do? How well did the forced changes of the Cultural Revolution work?**

2. **Why would the Red Guards worry so much about traditions and customs? What does this tell you about the importance of traditions and customs for the people who practise them?**

What Did People Think About the Cultural Revolution?

In the following conversation, you will read about how some people felt about the Cultural Revolution. Dai is a teacher and Song is a scientist. Both lived through the Cultural Revolution.

Song: *Every time I think about the Cultural Revolution, I feel very sad. It was 10 wasted years!*

Dai: *Yes, my university was closed for years. I wasn't able to complete my studies. I was sent to work on a farm in the country. My life has been wasted!*

Song: *I had just graduated from university in 1966. I ended up on a farm feeding pigs! The farmers hated us. What had we done wrong?*

Dai: *The people who got ahead were those who could repeat the words of Chairman Mao as though they really believed them. They tried to apply his teachings to everything!*

Song: *Many of them knew nothing about any subject. They thought the words of Chairman Mao could work magic!*

Dai: *My sister became a Red Guard. She and several others attacked their teachers. They made them kneel down and confess their "crimes"!*

Song: *Yes, their crimes were knowing foreign languages, or liking Western classical music. Only certain approved films and books were allowed in those days.*

Dai: *I remember. There were only a few approved operas, ballets, and films.*

Song: *They got pretty boring after you had seen them a dozen times!*

Dai: *The Red Guards thought they were wonderful, but these people were very young. They didn't know much about the real world.*

Song: *Even they were fed up in the end. When Chairman Mao ordered them to go to the frontiers to build the new China, they didn't want to go. Most of the Red Guards from the cities didn't know much about hard work. They were sent to places where there were no modern conveniences at all.*

Dai: *When the Cultural Revolution ended in 1976, we all realized how far China had fallen behind the rest of the world. We had to rush to catch up! We were all asked to come back from the countryside to help.*

Song: *Many of my friends were sent to other countries to improve their knowledge. Some went to Europe.*

Dai: *Many of my friends went, too. They went to Japan, the United States, or Canada. I was asked to teach school, but I'd been a farmer for a long, long time. I'd forgotten a lot of what I'd studied.*

Song: *As hard as we studied, we could not make up for the lost years.*

Dai: *What was worse, the Cultural Revolution produced many followers, but not many leaders.*

Song: *We can only hope that the new students will study hard and help China to modernize quickly.*

Dai: *And that their children will study even harder to make up for the 10 lost years of the Cultural Revolution.*

Song: *Already, the students are asking for more freedom and democracy. We can only watch and wait to see what happens.*

Modern China and the World

China has had many clashes with powerful countries in the past. Today, China is sensitive to the needs of weaker countries. It has often given them aid, and sought to defend their rights through international organizations like the United Nations.

The former Soviet Union became China's close friend because both countries had Communist governments. The Soviets helped China rebuild after the Second World War and the Chinese civil war that ended in 1949. They also sent experts to help shape the Chinese government. The two nations were friendly until 1960, when they argued over the proper way to govern people. Soviet experts went home and did not help the Chinese anymore.

In 1970, Canada opened an embassy in Beijing.

Likewise, the Chinese opened an embassy in Ottawa. After that, Canada and China began to trade. You have read about Canada selling wheat and other goods to China. You have also read about China selling tea and other goods to Canada. This kind of trade grew after 1970.

Many countries want to trade with the Chinese. They want to sell goods to China, because it has so many **consumers**. These countries also want to set up factories in China because Chinese wages are not very high. In turn, the Chinese want to sell goods to the world. They also hope trade will bring them the latest technologies from other countries.

In 1972, American president Richard Nixon went to meet Chairman Mao in Beijing. Since then, the United States and China have become quite friendly. The former Soviet Union, too, changed its policies toward China. By 1989, China and the Soviet Union were cooperating again.

Modern China is organized into provinces, autonomous regions, and municipalities. These political units are much like those in other large countries. In 1970, Canada opened an embassy in China's capital, Beijing.

A LOOK BACK

China's government, like Canada's, has changed in many ways over the years. Changes have occurred as the government tries to address the special problems of a large country with a huge population.

For thousands of years, China kept to itself. Eventually, contacts with other countries helped the Chinese to learn about new ways of doing things. Many people, especially Chinese students, wanted to apply these new ways to China. When the Communist government led by Mao Zedong came to power in 1949, many new ideas were introduced to the people of China.

The changes the Communists brought were many and sudden. All aspects of life in China were affected. Some changes affected the Chinese in positive ways, while others were negative. Changes during the Cultural Revolution were often painful for the Chinese. For many, the Cultural Revolution meant that they were no longer able to practise many of the traditions important to them.

The Cultural Revolution was an attempt to run China in a new way. Most people now agree that it failed. The Cultural Revolution kept China isolated from other countries. This isolation meant that many of the changes happening in other nations, such as Canada, did not occur in China. The Chinese missed the benefits that these changes brought to Canada and other nations. After Mao Zedong's death, the new government under Deng Xiaoping made changes that created stronger relations between China and other countries.

The Chinese are still trying to find the best way to govern their country. The people's need for more personal freedom makes the future of the Communist government uncertain. In the meantime, changes continue to occur. Relations with other countries, like Canada, may help bring positive change to the lives of the Chinese people.

A LOOK AHEAD

- Chapter 12 is a review of the main ideas found in each chapter of this textbook.

- You will be given the opportunity to compare the ways Chinese and Canadian people meet their needs.

Questions

1. Russia and the United States are powerful nations. Why do you think they are interested in China?

2. Canada and China are almost the same geographic size, but their governments are different. How are the governments of Canada and China the same? How are they different?

3. Give reasons why you think it is important for countries in the world to cooperate with one another. Discuss how this can contribute to world peace.

4. Do you think the Cultural Revolution was good or bad for the Chinese? Explain your answer.

Activities

1. In magazines and newspapers, find articles about some Pacific Rim neighbours. Look especially for articles about

   (a) Russia and China,

   (b) the United States and China, and

   (c) Canada and China.

   Add the articles to your notebook and record what you have learned about the relationships between these countries.

2. In the past, China viewed itself as superior to other nations. It was inward looking. Now it is outward looking. In groups of four or five, discuss what made China change its attitude.

CONCLUSION

Canada and China: Neighbours on the Pacific Rim

If you do not climb the mountain

You cannot view the plain

—Old Chinese Saying

CHAPTER FOCUS

Throughout this textbook, you have examined many aspects of China. This chapter concludes your study of China and reviews the main ideas presented in the areas of the Pacific Rim, geography, climate, people, family, education, lifestyles, and history. As you read, think about the ways in which China and Canada are the same yet different.

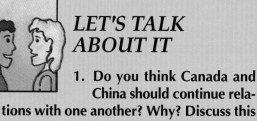

LET'S TALK ABOUT IT

1. Do you think Canada and China should continue relations with one another? Why? Discuss this in a group of four or five. Present your answer to the class.

In 1973, Canadian prime minister Trudeau visited China. Soon after, China and Canada became trading partners.

The Pacific Rim

Canada and China are the second and third largest countries in the world. Both countries border on the Pacific Ocean. They are neighbours on the Pacific Rim.

The idea of the Pacific Rim became popular in the 1970s and 1980s. This is when countries that share the Pacific Ocean as a common border started to trade more with one another. One result of this trade was people from these countries began to visit and learn more about each other.

Canadians want to know more about their Pacific Rim neighbours. We want to know how they live, what makes them laugh, what they like to eat, how they work, and how they play. One of the Pacific Rim countries you know more about now is China.

Geography

Although Canada and China are nearly the same size, their geography is different. Canada, for example, is a northern country. Most of its land is north of the 49th **parallel**. Most of China lies south of the 49th.

China has only one seacoast, along the Pacific Ocean. Canada has three seacoasts, along the Atlantic, Arctic, and Pacific oceans.

Each country has rugged mountains and flat plains. Two of China's rivers, the Huanghe and the Changjiang, are much longer than any in Canada. Canada, on the other hand, has lakes much larger than those in China.

Climate

China's climate is milder than Canada's. Most of Canada has snowfall in the winter. Only the far north of China is cold and has snow. The southern half of China rarely, if ever, has ice and snow. Canada's weather is affected by the snow and ice in its north. In China, weather is affected by huge deserts and monsoon winds. In general, Canadians must wear warmer clothing in all seasons than the Chinese.

Because of the differences in climate, China produces a much larger range of fruits and vegetables than does Canada. This has made Chinese food different from Canadian food. But we do share a number of crops in common, such as wheat, corn, potatoes, and sugarbeets.

People

Canada's and China's populations are different. To begin with, China's population is nearly 40 times greater than Canada's.

Both countries are home to peoples of different ethnic groups. In China, 92 per cent of the population is made up of one group, called the Han Chinese. The Han trace their roots back for thousands of years. The remaining population is made up of 55 different ethnic groups, who have lived in China for hundreds of years.

Canada's population is made up of many different groups of people, too. Canada's earliest peoples, the Native peoples, have been in Canada for thousands of years. Canada was settled by two main European groups, the English and the French. Today, however, the majority of new Canadians come from Asia. These immigrants are coming from places such as Hong Kong, India, the Philippines, Vietnam, and China.

Helping people of many backgrounds is a challenge the governments of China and Canada face regularly.

Family

In both Canada and China, the family is an important influence in society. But the role of the family in each country has been different. Traditionally, the family in China has been more important than its individual members. While this is changing, there are still many Chinese homes where three generations of one family live together. Their close relatives often live nearby. Most Canadians do not live with their parents or grandparents. Many Canadians move around the country, so families are often spread widely apart.

Education

Education is important in both China and Canada. Traditionally in China, only the wealthy could afford to be educated. Those who were clever enough to pass very difficult exams were then given important positions in government and society. Only in the 1900s was an effort made to make education available to more people.

The opportunity for higher education in Canada is much greater for the individual than it is in China. This is changing in China, however, as the need to modernize becomes greater.

China and Canada have cooperated in educational areas. Many Chinese students have come to Canada to study.

Lifestyles

While there are many differences in the way Canadians and Chinese live, there are also many things we have in common. A love of nature, of learning, and of friendship are but a few of those things. As Canadians and Chinese trade more, they will affect each other's lifestyles. For example, many Canadians drink Chinese tea, and many Chinese like to eat foods made from Canadian wheat.

History

China's history has spanned thousands of years. Rulers and dynasties have come and gone. There have been long periods of fighting and war in China's history, followed by periods of peace.

Canada's history as a single nation is much shorter than China's. There has been less fighting and more peaceful development in Canada.

Both China and Canada have had to learn how to interact with other countries. This was true historically. It will continue to be true in the future.

Changing China

Throughout this book, you found examples of how Chinese meet their needs. People change. So do countries! That's certainly true of both China and Canada. As people and countries change, they meet their basic needs in new ways. Once these basic needs are met, other needs, like the need to have certain household items, begin to become important. One of the main things to remember is people everywhere have the same basic needs for food, clothing, and shelter. In some cases, people in each country meet these needs in the same ways. Some reasons for people meeting their needs in different ways have to do with each country's geography.

Customs and traditions have played and continue to play an important role in the way Chinese meet their needs. One of the most important influences in Chinese life has been Confucianism, which influenced the way people thought and acted in the past. Other traditions, like honouring one's ancestors, have also influenced the way the Chinese live. But some traditions are changing. For example, most families now have only one child. As well, women are no longer considered inferior to men.

Because of its size, its rugged countryside, and its many peoples, communication has long been a challenge in China. Today, new technology has helped China meet the communication challenge. Technology like telephones and fax machines allows the Chinese to communicate with one another, and with their neighbours across the Pacific Ocean and around the world.

Technologies like Western medicine and Western farming practices make it easier for China to care for and feed its people. While China has learned more about Western ideas, it has also shared many of its own ideas, about acupuncture and communes, for example, with countries like Canada. It is almost always a good idea for countries to try and find ways they can share. Especially if they happen to be "neighbours"!

Activities

1. Return to the Think About It questions on page vii of this textbook.

   (a) Answer the questions again.

   (b) Compare your new answers to your previous ones.

   (c) How have your answers to these questions changed now that you have completed your study of China?

2. Look at the caption under the illustration on page x. What new information can you add to the list you had made at the beginning of your study?

Glossary

When you go **abroad**, you go outside your own country, especially overseas.

Your **ancestral village** is the place where your parents, grandparents, or earlier relatives were born.

Arable land is farmland. It is suitable for growing crops.

Archeologists look for the remains of cities, homes, monuments, and other artifacts of long-dead peoples. They use this archeological evidence to study the life and customs of ancient times.

An **armoire** is a large, decorated cabinet.

Authorities are the officials in control. An authority has the right to command or act.

Barbarians are people considered to be rude, savage, and lacking in knowledge.

Braziers are small heaters that burn coal or charcoal.

Child care is the term used for the ways that people care for their children's needs. Today, day-care centres are important for child care because they provide care and training while parents are at work.

City-states are cities that have their own governments and behave like a country. They look out for their own interests.

Civil servants are employees who do the day-to-day work of government.

Communes are communities of people who share living space, possessions, and responsibilities. The needs of all the people living in a commune are provided for by the commune itself.

The **Communists** in China follow a political belief system called communism. Communists believe that the wealth of a country should be shared. Mao Zedong led the Communist Party to power in China in 1949. He believed it was unfair that some people were very rich and powerful, while others were poor and hungry.

A **concubine** is a secondary wife. Concubines are found in societies where men have more than one wife. The concubine is considered less important than the first wife.

Consumers are people who buy and use food, clothing, or other goods and services.

Courtyards are spaces surrounded by walls. They have very high roofs, or no roofs at all. They are usually near or in a large building.

During the **Cultural Revolution** in China (1966-1976), people were told what to do and what to read. One goal of this revolution was to replace the old ways with the new, whether most Chinese approved or not.

The **Customs** office at an airport or border-crossing is the place where goods entering the country are checked.

The **customs** of a people are their long-established ways of doing things.

Daoism is an ancient Chinese religion that goes back 2500 years. It includes the teachings of the philosopher Laozi. Daoists believe in living a life in harmony with nature.

Deltas are the deposits of earth and sand that collect at the mouths of some rivers.

In a **democracy**, the government tries to treat everyone equally. People freely elect their government, and have rights such as freedom of speech.

Diplomatic relations are established between two countries when their governments agree to set up dealings with each other. For example, they open embassies in each other's countries, and discuss ways of helping one another.

The **dominant** group is the one that is most influential or powerful.

Droughts are long periods of dry weather.

A **dynasty** was created in China's past when a series of emperors came from the same family. For example, the Zhou Dynasty was a series of emperors who were members of the Zhou family. Dynasties mark important eras in China's history.

Economics is the study of how wealth is produced, distributed, and used.

An **economy** is the total of all the activities that produce wealth in a country. It is also the way a country manages its wealth.

An **elite** is a group of people considered special because of their education, wealth, or power.

An **endangered species** is a plant or animal that is threatened with extinction.

An **excavated** village is one that has been uncovered by digging. To excavate is to bring out of the ground something which has been buried.

To **export** is to send articles or goods out of one country for sale and use in another.

There is a **famine** when people in a certain place have little or nothing to eat.

Generations are all the people born at about the same time. Your parents belong to one generation, and you belong to the next generation.

Harmony is an agreement of feelings, ideas, or actions. It means all parts are working well together. For example, to prepare for the Chinese Lantern Festival, people work together to make giant lanterns for public display. This is an example of people working in harmony. However, the Chinese view of harmony is more than team work. It is also a state of mind. When the parts of a whole all fit together well, harmony is achieved.

The **Head Tax** was a fee that each Chinese person had to pay to enter Canada. This tax ended in 1923.

An **heir** is a person who inherits, or receives something after the original owner has died. An heir could inherit money, property, or authority.

Illiterate means unable to read or write.

Immigrants are people who move to a new country to live.

Inferior means lower in position or importance. In traditional China, women had a lower position than men.

The **intellectual class** in Confucian China was the group of rich men chosen to be taught by great teachers. Their role was to work with their minds, not their hands. They maintained the ideas and customs of traditional China.

Irrigation is used to supply water to dry land. Irrigation methods include using ditches and sprinklers.

Islam is the religion founded by the prophet Muhammad.

Lucky money is money that adults put in little red envelopes to give to children on their birthdays or at Spring Festival. This money is considered to be lucky. The children can spend it or save it.

Luxury items are things that make life more comfortable but are not necessary to live.

Martial arts train people in physical fitness, self-defence, and mental strength. Karate is an example of a martial art.

Matchmakers are people who arrange marriages for other people.

Minority groups are made up of people living in a country who are not part of the largest group of citizens.

To **modernize** means to use new ideas and techniques.

A **monsoon** is a wind that changes direction with the seasons. It blows in India, China, and other Southeast Asian countries. Winter monsoons are usually dry. Summer monsoons bring large amounts of rain.

Mosques are the places where Muslims worship.

Muslims are followers of Muhammad and the Islamic religion. They believe that Allah is the only God.

Navigators are the people who determine the position, course, and distance traveled by a ship, aircraft, or spacecraft.

The **One Child policy** was introduced in China in 1979. The government rewards people for having only one child. The goal is to reduce the large size of China's population.

Opium is a powerful drug that causes sleep, eases pain, and can affect a person's behaviour. It is made from a kind of poppy. People who use it become addicted to it.

The **Pacific Rim** is made up of all the countries that have a coast along the Pacific Ocean. Pacific Rim neighbours share the Pacific coast from north to south and east to west.

A **palaeontological** expedition would be one in which scientists search for fossils of animals and plants. Palaeontology is the science that studies fossils to learn about different life forms that lived long ago.

A **parallel** is an imaginary circle around the Earth that marks a degree of latitude.

Peasants are people who live in the country and work the land for a landowner. They usually do not own the land they work on, and are often poor.

The **Peking Man** was a prehistoric human that used stone tools and fire.

Philosophers are people who have created a set of principles about the nature of human-kind and the universe.

Profits are the gains from a business. Traders from other countries who came to China wanted to buy Chinese goods, such as silk. These could be sold in their home countries for more money than was paid, creating a profit.

Prosperity is another word for success or good fortune.

A **quota** is the amount or number of goods that people are expected to make, or are allowed to make, or are required to make. For example, if a farm has a quota of grain, this means the government has told the farmer how much grain to grow.

To take **refuge** is to protect yourself by taking shelter, safe from danger.

If something is **regulated**, it is controlled by rules.

A **republic** is a country in which the citizens elect the government. It has no king, queen, or appointed leaders.

A **revered** possession is one that is deeply cherished and respected.

Revolts are fights in which people rebel against their government or leaders.

Rituals are solemn ceremonies.

A **seismograph** is a device that records the length, direction, and intensity of earthquakes.

Sophisticated means experienced and advanced in knowledge.

To **succeed**, in this instance, means to take the place of the person before you.

A **surplus** is an amount over and above what is needed.

Switchboards are panels containing switches and meters that open and close circuits. A telephone switchboard has plugs for connecting one telephone line to another.

The **tablet** in Grandmother Chen's apartment is a small, flat slab of wood that has family names carved or painted on it.

Technology is the application of science in practical ways. It involves using materials, tools, machines, techniques, and know-how to produce goods and services.

Tinder is anything that catches fire easily.

Traditions are the beliefs, opinions, and customs that are passed on from one generation to another.

A **translator** is a person who changes words from one language into another.

Twinned towns, cities, provinces, or even schools in one country set up ties with those in another country. Places that are twinned learn about each other.

Typhoons are violent storms with spiraling winds that form over the Pacific Ocean.

A **tyrannical** ruler is one who uses power cruelly and unjustly.

Value is a quality people feel is most important.

Western ideas are ideas from Europe or America. They are sometimes different from ideas from Asia.

Pronunciation Guide

The Chinese Pinyin System

The Chinese Phonetic Alphabet (CPA) uses letters from the Latin alphabet to show the pronunciation of Chinese characters. Chinese characters are not phonetic symbols. By using a phonetic symbol in the form of Latin alphabet, you can sound out the Chinese word.

The following chart shows the CPA and its sounds in English.

CPA	English sound	Example
a	a	father
ai	ai	eye
ao	au	now
b	b	bay
c	ts	hats
ch	ch	church
d	d	day
e	e	her
ei	ei	eight
er	er	err
f	f	fay
g	g	good
h	h	hay

CPA	English sound	Example
i, yi	i, y,yi	see
ia, ya	ya	Asia
iao, yao	yau	miao
ie, ye	ye	yes
j	j	jet
k	k	key
l	l	lay
m	m	may
n	n	nay
ng	ng	sing
o	o	saw
ong	ung	lung
ou	ou	oh
p	p	pay
q	ch	church
r	r	leisure
s	s	say
sh	sh	shirt
t	t	tea
u	u	rude
ü	yu, yw	you
ua, wa	wa	guano
uai, wai	wai	wife
üe	we	we
uo, wo	wo	wall
x	sy	she
z	dz	reads
zh	j	judge

Index

Credits

Editorial: Nancy Mackenzie, Leah-Ann Lymer, Carolyn Pogue-Phipps, Melanie Johnson, Jennifer Keane

Typesetting & Design: Pièce de Résistance Ltée., Edmonton, AB

Illustrations: Yu Chao and Wang Jue

Maps: Johnson Cartographics, Edmonton, AB

Lithography: Neville Lomberg

Printing: Quality Color Press, Edmonton, AB

Index: Adrian Mather

Photos: Brian Evans

Additional Photos:

Entries are by page number, coded as follows:
T = Top B = Bottom R = Right L = Left

6   TR-British Columbia Archives and Records Service/HP93307
7   Courtesy Paul Tawrell
12   BR-Courtesy Air China, Vancouver, BC
54   TL-Canadian International Development Agency/Photo by Gary Chapman
60   B-Agnes Yu
71   BR-Courtesy Carolyn Pogue-Phipps

We have made every effort to correctly identify and credit the sources of all photographs, illustrations, and information used in this textbook. Reidmore Books appreciates any further information or corrections; acknowledgment will be given in subsequent editions.